Design and History

In 1897, the Norddeutscher Lloyd liner *Kaiser Wilhelm der Grosse* entered service on the North Atlantic run. Compared with other German liners of the era, this ship was different. In fact, compared with all liners crossing the Atlantic on regular passages, this ship was different. She was built by a German yard, she was the largest ship in the world, and she soon proved herself to be the fastest, and she was the first four-funnelled liner.

The North Atlantic trade had been dominated by Britain. Cunard had two record breakers, *Lucania* and *Campania*, in service, so the new German-built wonderliner came as a shock to the British and, for the fastest transatlantic passenger ship voyage, she won the prestigious Blue Riband on her fourth trip. This was the first time that the distinction went to a German ship.

In the ten years starting in 1897, Norddeutscher Lloyd built four four-funnelled liners and Hamburg Amerika Linie built one – *Deutschland*, which in 1900 took the Blue Riband from *Kaiser Wilhelm der Grosse*.

However, these high-speed liners all had two fundamental flaws: they were expensive to run and they vibrated badly, particularly towards the stern, where it was most uncomfortable for passengers. Nevertheless, these German successes were a blow to the British.

The second blow to British shipping came when the prestigious Oceanic Steam Navigation Co Ltd, better known as White Star Line, was sold to the International Mercantile Marine Company (IMMC), or in other words John Pierpont Morgan, the American financier and banker. Even though White Star Line ships continued to sail under the British flag, were manned by British crews and the headquarters remained in England, the White Star Line was owned in the United States.

The British needed to respond. In 1907, Cunard commissioned *Lusitania* and *Mauretania*. These too would both win the Blue Riband, and *Mauretania* would remain the fastest ship on the North Atlantic until 1929, when the Blue Riband was recaptured, again, by Germany.

DESIGN BACKGROUND

On a summer evening in 1907, J Bruce Ismay, chairman of White Star Line, and Lord Pirrie, chairman of Harland & Wolff, the Belfast shipbuilders, met at Pirrie's home at Belgrave Square in London. The topic of the conversation was no doubt the developments in the transatlantic business. The idea of two giant liners, with possibly a third to follow and destined to win back passenger trade for White Star, was born over after-dinner drinks and cigars. These two giant liners would be named *Olympic*

Taken on 31 May 1911, this photo depicts a gala day for Harland & Wolff as in addition to the successful launch of the *Titanic*, her sister *Olympic* was handed over to her owners. On board the little *Nomadic* in the foreground is Bruce Ismay, chairman of the White Star Line, and Lord Pirrie, chairman of Harland & Wolff and other distinguished guests being ferried out to the *Olympic*, which was waiting in the River Lagan to begin her first crossing to Liverpool. *Nomadic* was built as one of two tenders (the second was the *Traffic*) to ferry passengers from Cherbourg harbour to the *Olympic* class liners berthed outside as they were too large for docking inside the harbour.

Olympic being launched on 10 October 1910 at Harland & Wolff's shipyard in Belfast. For reasons unknown the hull of the *Olympic* was painted white for the launch; *Titanic*'s hull was painted dark grey and *Britannic*'s medium grey. Some historians suggest this was to make the ships distinguishable in black-and-white photographs.

and *Titanic*. No attempt would be made to surpass the new Cunarders and the German record breakers in speed. Speed was not of the essence. These two new ships would be outstanding in size, luxury, comfort and safety with features such as electric lifts, an indoor swimming pool and a gymnasium. The lesser speed would lead to less vibration and so, in turn, improve passenger comfort. The gross tonnage of each liner was to be 45,000, which was considerably larger than the new Cunarders. A third ship, *Gigantic*, would follow.

They were to be powered by a combination of two four-cylinder triple-expansion reciprocating engines for the wing propellers and a Parsons low-pressure turbine for the centre propeller. This combination had been tried and tested on White Star's *Laurentic* and it proved to be very economical. The machinery was to be fired by twenty-four double-ended boilers with six furnaces each and five single-ended boilers with three furnaces each. *Titanic*'s reciprocating engines, the largest ever built, extended over four decks and two watertight compartments.

Despite the disaster on 14 April 1912, *Titanic* was possibly the safest ship of her time. Her hull was divided into sixteen watertight compartments and had a double bottom. By the 'flick of a switch' the captain could close the watertight doors and make

the vessel 'practically unsinkable'. She could stay afloat with her first three watertight compartments opened to the sea. Indeed, *Titanic* would have remained afloat if she had hit the iceberg head on, but nobody foresaw a glancing blow that would open six watertight compartments to fatally wound the ship and cause her to founder.

Nor was it ever intended to leave the third class passengers to their fate. The idea behind so few lifeboats was that there would always be a ship nearby to assist should something happen. The idea was to row out the first class passengers first, row back to collect the second class and then the third. This philosophy was supported by the experience gained during the loss of the White Star's *Republic*, which sank in 1909 after a collision in heavy fog. *Republic*'s wireless operator sent out the first CQD in history and several ships came to *Republic*'s assistance. The few casualties were a direct result of the collision. Nearly everyone on board was saved.

On 28 July 1908, a delegation of the most important people in British shipping arrived at Harland & Wolff's shipyard at Queen's Island, Belfast. Harland & Wolff had prepared concept plans and a small half-model of the giant new ships. With Morgan's financial muscle in the background, the costs of these ships would clearly be covered. Three days later, on 31 July, the contract letter was signed for the two liners – the builder's yard numbers 400 (*Olympic*) and 401 (*Titanic*). *Olympic*'s keel was laid on 16 December 1908, followed by *Titanic*'s just over three months later on 31 March 1909. This time span was necessary to take some of the logistical pressure off the workshops during the construction of these huge ships.

In the unpredictable weather of spring 1909, the cellular double bottom of *Titanic* expanded from each side of the keel. During the summer months the workers began to raise the frames. *Titanic*'s hull was fully framed by April 1910 and work on the hull plating began. The shell plates were generally about 30 ft long and up to 6 ft high. The largest plates each weighed 4.5 tons. Mild steel was used for construction throughout.

Above the bridge deck, the upper hull was built of lighter scantlings and was of lesser structural significance. Two expansion joints were included into these decks to permit the hull to move and flex freely when the ship was under way in heavy seas.

The shell plates were kept together by steel rivets that could easily fit into the palm of a man's hand, and which were pushed through holes in overlapping shell plates. The end of the rivet shaft that extended beyond the overlapping plates was hydraulically compressed into a snap (rounded) head in a split second. This action fired the rivet red-hot and as it cooled it shrank and thereby pulled the overlapping shell plates tight. Three million rivets were needed to build each hull. By October 1910, the shell plating was complete.

Olympic was launched on 20 October 1910 and she was moored at the deep-water wharf where fitting out began. Her hull settled deeper into the water as the boilers were installed, funnels and masts were erected and the superstructure, winches and vents were bolted onto her decks.

The last day of May 1911 was memorable for Harland & Wolff and White Star Line, because on this day *Olympic* was handed over to her owners and *Titanic* was successfully launched. It was also Lord Pirrie's birthday. A large number of distinguished guests were invited by Harland & Wolff to witness the launch of its greatest ship yet – *Titanic*. In beautiful weather the guests on board the chartered Irish Sea ferry *Duke of Argyll* saw the glistening new *Olympic* in all her splendour as they steamed past her on their way from Liverpool to Belfast early that morning. As usual at Harland & Wolff there was no naming ceremony. To warn small craft to stay well clear, at 12.05pm, two rockets were fired and these were followed a few

Rivet detail of the *Olympic* can be seen to advantage in the Thompson dry-dock in Belfast. The unscreened open promenade deck can be seen, as well as the arrangement of B-deck windows, two of the significant details making the *Olympic* and the *Titanic* distinguishable. The second funnel has already been painted.

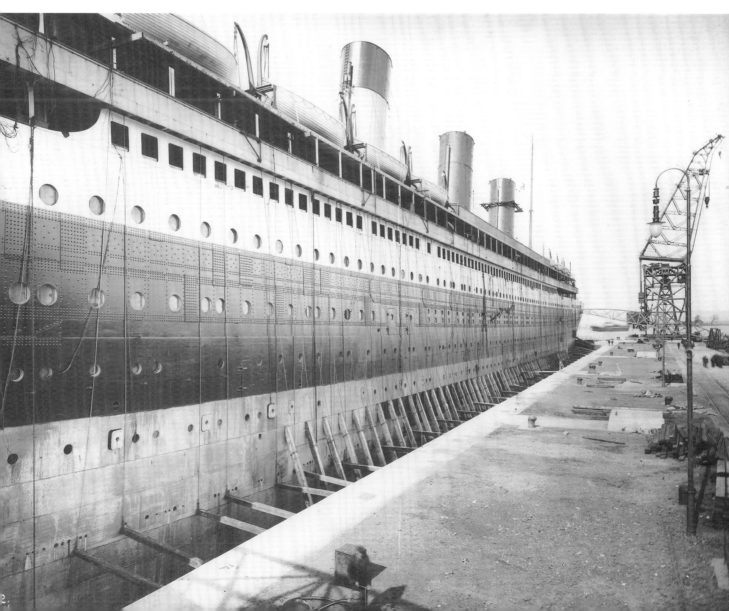

minutes later by a third. After the launching triggers had been fired, *Titanic's* hull began to move down the ways under its own weight. Thousands of spectators cheered as the hull slid backwards into the River Lagan just after midday.

After reaching a speed of 12 knots and having travelled some 500 metres, the hull was stopped by six anchors and two 80-ton drag chains. Workers removed the anchor cables from the hull and tugs towed *Titanic* to the deep water wharf to be fitted out.

At 2.30pm, *Nomadic* left Belfast to join *Olympic*. On board were, among others, J P Morgan, J Bruce Ismay, Lord Pirrie and other notables from Harland & Wolff and White Star Line. At 4.30pm, *Olympic*, under the command of Captain Edward J Smith, Commodore of White Star Line, left for Liverpool a mere twenty-nine months after her keel was laid and, even more astonishing, seven-and-a-half months after fitting out had begun. After arrival in Liverpool on 1 June, she was opened to the public. Shortly before midnight on the same day, she left for Southampton from where she would embark on her maiden voyage on 14 June. After a day's trip, *Olympic* arrived at Southampton before daylight on 3 June 1911 and preparations for the maiden voyage began immediately. She was again opened to the public in Southampton on 10 June.

OLYMPIC ENTERS SERVICE

The crew mustered at 8.00am on 14 June on board *Olympic* and slowly the passengers began to arrive, adding to the excitement of the pre-voyage activity. Shortly after midday, *Olympic* was towed backwards out of her berth and she began her maiden voyage to Cherbourg, Queenstown and New York with a full complement of passengers. Thousands had come to see her off. It was a gala occasion and *Olympic* was on every front page.

Although the voyage was hampered by poor weather, it was highly successful for White Star Line. *Olympic* had logged a speed of over 21 knots, although her five single-ended boilers remained unfired for the whole crossing. After reaching New York, Ismay cabled to Pirrie 'Olympic is a marvel! She has given unbounded satisfaction! Once again receive my warmest and most sincere congratulations!' During this trip, Ismay had carefully noted improvements of the design that could be included on *Titanic*. One of his observations was that the promenade space on B-deck was too large and hardly used by passengers. As a consequence, the same area on *Titanic* received additional staterooms.

Cunard Line had been watching White Star's new ships and had decided that if it wanted to remain in business it would need its own version of the 'wonderships'.

Only a few days after *Titanic* was launched the keel plates were laid for the Cunard liner *Aquitania*.

In Germany, Hamburg Amerika Linie already had the 50,000-ton *Europa* under construction (it would eventually be named *Imperator*) and two more ships, *Vaterland* and *Bismarck*, were to follow.

White Star Line had no time to rest on its laurels. With three ships, it could offer a

Nomadic is alongside *Olympic* on the day of her being handed over to her owners the White Star Line on 31 May 1911 – the day the *Titanic* was launched. After the guests had boarded the *Olympic*, Captain E J Smith, Commodore of the White Star Line, took command of the *Olympic* for her crossing to Liverpool and then for her maiden voyage from Southampton to New York on 14 June 1911.

weekly service between Southampton and New York, instead of the fortnightly service with two ships. After the success of *Olympic*'s maiden voyage, minds were made up and the order for *Gigantic* (Harland & Wolff Yard No 433) confirmed, but her keel was not laid until November 1911 because the slip, the same on which *Olympic* was built, was occupied at the time. *Olympic* returned to Southampton on 5 July after reaching a speed of 22.32 knots on this eastbound run; all of her boilers were lit and weather conditions were more favourable.

On her next passages, *Olympic* began to settle into the routine as a transatlantic liner. It was not until her fifth trip to New York that liners of such size became a cause for concern. She had left Southampton for New York on the morning of 20 September and was approaching the Bramble Bank when the cruiser HMS *Hawke* was spotted to her starboard side approaching from the Solent. After *Olympic* had rounded the Bank both ships were heading for Spithead, the channel north-east of the Isle of Wight, and were on a near parallel course when *Hawke* suddenly turned to port as if to pass *Olympic* astern.

However, the cruiser smashed into *Olympic*'s starboard side directly beneath the aft well deck and almost capsized; it left a gaping hole in the liner's side. The sheer momentum of the gigantic liner tore off *Hawke*'s ram and the cruiser span around like a top as she was finally released from the liner that was speeding past her. Several second-class cabins were demolished but fortunately there were no casualties, because most of the passengers were

Maiden Arrival in New York on a hot summer's day in June 1911. The crew is busy unloading cargo and one crewman is taking advantage of the heat by hanging up his washing on the railing. Some crew members are taking a break in the forward well deck.

■ *OLYMPIC*

Length (overall):	882.75 ft (269.05 m)
Length (between perpendiculars):	852.4 ft (259.8 m)
Breadth:	92.5 ft (28.19 m)
Draught (loaded):	34.6 ft (10.54 m)
Tonnages (as built):	45,324 gross, 20,847 net
Machinery:	Two four-cylinder triple-expansion reciprocating steam engines fed by twenty-four double-ended and five single-ended Scotch boilers and each producing 15,000 indicated horsepower for two wing propellers. One Parsons low-pressure turbine producing 15,000 shaft horsepower for central four-blade propeller.
Speed:	21 knots (service), 22.82 knots (maximum)
Passenger accommodation (as built):	735 (1st class), 674 (2nd), 1026 (3rd)

Above: *Titanic* being fitted out in the Harland & Wolff fitting out basin.

Above, right: *Titanic* during fitting out

Below: *Titanic*'s sea-trials were postponed for one day due to gale force winds.

in the dining saloon having lunch. However, the crossing was cancelled.

Due to tidal considerations, *Olympic* could not return to Southampton. Immediately after the collision she anchored in Osborne Bay and later steamed on to Cowes, where the passengers were taken off by tenders. The following day, *Olympic* slowly steamed back to Southampton where the gash was sealed with wooden patches and on 3 October she

headed for Belfast to be repaired. Travelling at very low speed, she arrived there three days later.

Harland & Wolff was already experiencing difficulties in keeping the construction of *Titanic* on schedule and this was made worse with *Olympic* arriving back in the yard for repairs. *Olympic* went back into service on 29 November 1911. On 25 September, White Star Line announced that the date for *Titanic*'s maiden voyage would be 20 March 1912. However, after *Olympic* had arrived in Belfast for repairs, it was announced that the departure date for *Titanic* would be 10 April 1912.

Olympic's series of misfortunes was not over. On 24 February 1912, while on her way to Southampton from New York, she lost a propeller blade and had to return to Belfast yet again for repairs, and again it had an adverse effect on the schedule for *Titanic*'s completion.

TITANIC'S MAIDEN VOYAGE

As one of the final changes in the construction of *Titanic*, the forward promenade deck sides were enclosed because experience with *Olympic* had shown that this area had a tendency to be wet in heavy seas. This

enclosure was one of the most significant visual differences between the two ships. While final touches were hastily made to *Titanic*, the officers and crew began to arrive at Belfast. Most of them lived on the ship while they became familiar with the equipment they would have to work with in the future. Time constraints did not permit *Titanic* to be opened to the public.

On 31 March, although some minor work was still being carried out, *Titanic* was ready for sea trials that were to begin the following day, but the weather turned out to be most unfavourable and trials were post-poned to 2 April. Time was running out!

At 6.00am on 2 April, which was a clear day, four tugs manoeuvred the liner out of the dock and from Belfast Lough into the open sea. Smoke pouring from *Titanic*'s first three funnels indicated that furnaces were being fired. A short distance before Carrickfergus the tugs dropped their tow ropes and the trials could begin. At 6.00pm, after completing the trials and returning to Belfast, a representative from the British Board of Trade, Francis Carruthers, who had been following the trials, instructed one more final test: both anchors were to be dropped and raised. After all trials had proven satisfactory, Carruthers signed the certificate clearing *Titanic* for use for transatlantic passenger transportation. Afterwards Thomas Andrews, representing Harland & Wolff, handed over *Titanic* to her owners, represented by Harold Sanderson.

All crew members who were not to travel

to Southampton disembarked and shortly after 8.00pm *Titanic* left Belfast heading for Southampton. Final preparations and tests were still being carried out on board, and on this trip *Titanic* reached a little more than 23 knots – the highest speed she would ever log. After midnight on 3 April 1912, at high tide, *Titanic* reached Southampton, twelve hours after *Olympic* had left for another crossing to New York. Tugs carefully nudged her, stern first, into Berth 44 from where she would depart for her maiden voyage on 10 April.

Due to a coal strike, seamen could not find work on liners because these did not have enough coal to make their crossings. Some seamen had not worked for more than six weeks. Clearly, vacancies on *Titanic* were much sought after. Most were happy to sign on under the popular Captain Edward J Smith and particularly on the new *Titanic*. Most of the crew was signed on 6 April. The majority came from Southampton, others from Belfast, Liverpool and London. The coal dispute was settled on 6 April, which was too late to supply *Titanic* with the fuel needed for the journey across the Atlantic if she was to depart on schedule. Coal was taken from other IMMC ships berthed at Southampton. Their trips were cancelled and their passengers were transferred from these ships to *Titanic*.

On 5 April, Good Friday, *Titanic* was dressed overall. Colourful flags were fastened to *Titanic*'s lines from stem to

Titanic in the new Thompson dry-dock at Harland & Wolff early 1912. The ship had been moved from the fitting out basin so work could be carried out beneath the waterline. The remains of the launching-cradle were removed and the hull finally painted with anti-fouling-red. The promenade deck is as yet still unscreened. Shortly before completion decisions were made to enclose the forward half of the promenade deck as experience on board the *Olympic* had shown that this space had a tendency to be wet in heavy seas. This forward enclosure of the promenade deck increased *Titanic*'s gross tonnage, making her the largest ship in the world, although in dimensions *Olympic* and *Titanic* were the same size.

■ *TITANIC*

Length (overall):	882.75 ft (269.05 m)
Length (between perpendiculars):	852.5 ft (259.83 m)
Breadth:	92.5 ft (28.19 m)
Draught (loaded):	34.5 ft (10.54 m)
Tonnages:	46,329 gross, 21,831 net
Machinery:	Two four-cylinder triple-expansion reciprocating steam engines fed by twenty-four double-ended and five single-ended Scotch boilers and each producing 15,000 indicated horsepower for two wing propellers. One Parsons low-pressure turbine producing 15,000 shaft horsepower for central four-blade propeller.
Speed:	21 knots (service), 23 knots (maximum)
Passenger accommodation (as built):	1034 (1st class), 510 (2nd), 1022 (3rd)

stern for the enjoyment of the people of Southampton. Thomas Andrews was on board taking care of final details. He noted everything from defective heating fans to the number of screws on hat hooks in the staterooms.

At last, on 10 April, came the day of departure. The blue ensign (the captain was a Royal Navy Reserve officer) was hoisted at the stern and at 6.00am the crew began to come on board. Bruce Ismay and his family had spent the night at the South Western Hotel. He could see *Titanic* from his hotel room. Mrs Ismay and their children did not make the crossing, but were given a tour of the ship while she was still at Southampton.

A surveyor from the British Board of Trade was on board undertaking final inspections. Boats 11 and 15 were lowered and raised again. Once this had been completed, the surveyor went to the bridge to Captain Smith. The lowering of the boats was completed to the surveyor's satisfaction and he signed his report verifying that he had seen a satisfactory boat drill and that *Titanic* had bunkered sufficient coal to take her to New York. In return, Captain Smith handed him the 'Masters Report to Company', stating that his ship was

prepared and serviceable. They shook hands and the surveyor wished Captain Smith good luck. Shortly afterwards Bruce Ismay and Thomas Andrews arrived on the bridge and congratulated Smith on his command.

The train with second class passengers had left Waterloo Station bound for Southampton at 7.30am. It arrived at Southampton two hours later and passengers boarded *Titanic* immediately. The corridors were crammed with passengers from all over Europe, finding their way to their cabins. The train carrying first class passengers left London at 9.45 and arrived at Southampton at 11.30am.

At noon, the sound of *Titanic*'s whistles boomed across Southampton and her one and only voyage began. As the ship got under way, the wake caused the liner *New York*, which was berthed nearby, to snap her mooring cables and its stern was drawn towards the passing *Titanic*. Only by quick reactions of the assisting tugs and by Captain Smith ordering full astern was a collision avoided. The first port of call was Cherbourg in France and then Queenstown in Ireland the next day to take on board further passengers and mail.

With 2240 people on board, *Titanic* set course for New York. She would never arrive

Opposite, top: *Titanic* leaving Belfast. She would never return. She is still very high in the water as further provisions such as china, silverware, bedclothes, food and drink etc. was taken onboard in Southampton.

Opposite, bottom: *Titanic* escorted out of Belfast harbour by tugs for sea trials on 2 April 1912.

Below: *Titanic* at Cherbourg on 10 April 1912. *Nomadic* and *Traffic*, even though not to be seen in this image, would be ferrying passengers out to the *Titanic*, whose size prevented her mooring inside the harbour.

Right: Dramatic bow view of *Olympic* entering New York harbour for the first time in June 1911. The paint on her bows eroded by heavy seas is a sign of a fairly rough crossing.

Far right: April 1912 view of *Olympic*, this time in Southampton. The same view of the *Titanic* would have been almost identical.

Olympic's steam whistles as attached to all four funnels. Those on the third and fourth funnel were perfectly identical dummies.

there. On the night of 14 April 1912, *Titanic* struck an iceberg and sank on 15 April at 2.20am with the loss of 1500 people. The most appalling maritime disaster in peacetime led to vast improvements of laws and regulations regarding the safety of life at sea. On the night of the sinking, the eastbound *Olympic*, under the command of Captain H J Haddock received distress calls from her sister but was too far away to come to her assistance.

Olympic, like *Titanic*, did not carry enough lifeboats to rescue all on board. After her arrival in Southampton she was hastily equipped with further collapsible lifeboats. Some of these were in poor condition. *Olympic* was due to leave

Southampton bound for New York at noon on 24 April. Ten minutes before the scheduled departure, men were seen to leave the vessel with their kit and using the aft gangway. They were not at all happy with the additional safety measures that White Star Line had installed in all of its ships. *Olympic* had been provided with twenty-four Berthon collapsible boats in addition to her usual complement of boats. These had been tried and tested under supervision of Commander Clarke from the Board of Trade. The liner finally left Ocean Dock at 1.30pm to clear the berth and went to an anchorage off Ryde, Isle of Wight, to await a fresh crew. Engineers kept the furnaces burning in the meantime. However, early the following day, *Olympic* was still at anchor and could not proceed on her voyage, although one hundred fireman had arrived from Portsmouth and were ready to join the liner. A demonstration of the effectiveness of the Berthon collapsibles was given before a delegation of the Seamen's Union. The remaining crew on *Olympic* agreed to commence work on the condition that one of the collapsibles, that had shown a slight leakage after two hours afloat, would be replaced.

But the bickering was not over yet. Some of the firemen decided not to return to *Olympic* unless the firemen who had remained loyal were dismissed from their charges. White Star firmly refused this and a new allotment of firemen was shipped to the awaiting *Olympic*. This made matters even worse. Soon afterwards most of the seamen abandoned *Olympic* on the same tender that had ferried the new firemen across on the grounds that the new firemen were not firemen at all. Finally, the crossing was cancelled on Friday and *Olympic* had to return to Southampton.

Fifty-three of *Olympic*'s crew were arrested. The charge was that 'they jointly,

and boiler rooms. She also received a 'Café Parisienne' and her *a la carte* restaurant was widened to make it similar to the restaurant on *Titanic*. In March 1913, she resumed service once again as the largest ship in the world. She would keep this title briefly because in June 1913 Hamburg Amerika Linie launched its *Imperator*, which exceeded the size of the *Olympic* class liners.

Left: *Olympic* lowering a lifeboat during the court investigations following the *Titanic* disaster.

BRITANNIC AND *OLYMPIC* AT WAR

The third of this trio of great liners was launched on 26 February 1914. Following the lessons learned in the sinking of *Titanic* and the Inquiry's recommendations, drastic design changes were made to *Britannic*. The most extreme change was the installation of a huge new davit arrangement, each designed to hold six lifeboats and even reach lifeboats on the opposite side of the ship, providing the funnel stays were not in the way. *Britannic*'s hull was 2 feet wider than the hulls of her sisters. Although it

being seamen engaged in the steamship *Olympic*, lying off Stokes Bay, did wilfully disobey the lawful commands of the Captain on the 26th instant.' They remained on bail for a week. When this action took place, *Olympic* had a total boat accommodation for 2514 persons – 200 more than were on board at the time.

After this occurrence, *Olympic*'s senior surgeon, Dr J C H Beaumont, described the 1912 seaman as follows:

> Firemen, in my experience, as a group, were ignorant, stubborn, impulsive, unreasoning and easily swayed by any agitator. He only had to voice a supposed grievance for the men to follow him like a flock of sheep, often not knowing what they are striking for.

In addition to the *Titanic* disaster and the appalling loss of life involved, this was beyond doubt one further mishap White Star could have easily lived without.

In October, *Olympic* returned to Harland & Wolff to be refitted. Apart from receiving sixty-four wooden lifeboats, the watertight bulkheads were raised up to B-deck and a double skin was constructed in the engine

The ship that never was: RMS *Britannic* depicted on a contemporary postcard as a transatlantic liner.

■ *BRITANNIC*

Length (overall):	882.75 ft (269.05 m)
Length (between perpendiculars):	852.5 ft (259.83 m)
Breadth:	94.5 ft (28.8 m)
Draught (loaded):	34.5 ft (10.54 m)
Tonnages:	48,158 gross, 53,147 displacement
Machinery:	Two four-cylinder triple-expansion reciprocating steam engines fed by twenty-four double-ended and five single-ended Scotch boilers and each producing 16,000 indicated horsepower for two wing propellers. One low-pressure turbine producing 18,000 shaft horsepower for central four-blade propeller.
Speed:	22 knots (service), 23 knots (maximum)
Passenger accommodation (intended):	2573 in three classes
Accommodation (as completed):	3309 military patients

Opposite: *Olympic*'s rudder and screw propellers. Recent research has shown that the propeller bosses were painted with the same anti-fouling red that was used to protect the hull from corrosion and marine-growth.

Right: The Harland & Wolff builders model of the *Britannic*, most likely at the World Trade Fair in Brussels in 1913. This model is still in existence and is on display at the Merseyside Maritime Museum in Liverpool, more or less altered to represent the *Titanic*.

was always denied by the White Star Line, early publicity brochures state that *Britannic* was to be given the name *Gigantic*. It was probably felt by some, that after the loss of *Titanic* this might be pushing their luck too far.

The outbreak of the First World War on 4 August 1914 would bring *Olympic* into a role for which she was never planned, but in which she would surely prove herself. *Olympic* was steaming west-bound when Captain Haddock was informed of the

outbreak of hostilities. On the return trip in October 1914 there were very few passengers on board due to the German U-boat threat. Towards the end of the voyage, *Olympic* was alerted that U-boats were awaiting her in English waters and she was ordered to divert to Glasgow. On 27 October, *Olympic* received distress calls from the battleship HMS *Audacious*, which had struck a mine off Tory Island and was sinking. After most of her crew had been taken on board *Olympic*, several attempts

Britannic being launched on 26 February 1914. She would never fly the White Star colours.

H1513.
R.W.

Copyright in Canada
McAskill.

S.S. Olympic
At No 2 Pier, Halifax

Olympic as a troop transport in Canada. She carried troops from Canada in the years 1915-17. These big liners proved to be too expensive to run as auxiliary cruisers and were instead used as hospital ships and troop transports for which they were perfect. Note the gun-platform that has been erected ahead of the foremast.

were made to tow the ship but all failed and at 8.55pm an explosion was heard on *Audacious* and she finally sank. This was witnessed and even photographed by passengers on board *Olympic* and because the Admiralty feared that news of the sinking would have a demoralising effect on the British public, the ship was held in custody at Lough Swilly, where passengers were not allowed to leave. Finally, on 2 November, *Olympic* arrived at Belfast, where the passengers disembarked.

In May 1915, *Britannic* completed her mooring trials and was made ready for requisition by the Admiralty and prepared for entry into service.

Olympic was to be laid up until the end of the war (at this point everybody said 'It will all be over by Christmas'). However, in September 1915, *Olympic* was requisitioned as a fast troop transport and in November *Britannic* as a hospital ship. Repainted white with a green band running the entire length of her hull interrupted by three large red crosses on both sides, HMHS *Britannic* was under the command of Captain Charles Bartlett. *Britannic*'s maiden voyage began on 23 December 1915 to the Mediterranean island of Lemnos. Many great liners were involved in the Gallipoli campaign, landing troops, but as casualties mounted the need for hospital ships rose. *Aquitania*, first in service as a

troop transport, was also requisitioned for duty as a hospital ship.

Up to November 1916, *Britannic* had made five successful trips to the Mediterranean evacuating the sick and wounded; she started her sixth trip on 12 November. *Britannic* had passed Gibraltar and after putting in to Naples was steaming at full speed into the Kea Channel when at 8.12am on 21 November a large explosion shook the ship. She had struck a mine on her starboard side between holds two and three, about 150 feet from the bow. The first four watertight compartments were filling rapidly when the order was given to close the watertight doors. However, the ship was wracked by further violent explosions, believed to have been coal dust exploding in her bunkers, and this caused massive contingent damage and disabled the automatic system for shutting the watertight doors. Distress signals were sent and the crew was ordered to prepare the lifeboats for lowering. To make matters worse, portholes had been left open to air the cabins (this was strictly forbidden) and as the ship listed to starboard water began to enter the hull here too.

Like her ill-fated sister, *Britannic* would never complete a commercial voyage to New York. At 9.07am, she sank with the loss of thirty lives. Had *Britannic* been on a home-bound voyage instead of outbound when she struck the mine, loaded with wounded and injured, the casualties would have been in the hundreds, if not thousands.

The sole survivor of the three sisters, *Olympic*, continued to transport troops to the Mediterranean until March 1916, when she was ordered to Liverpool. Her future was uncertain at that time but the Canadian government stepped in and chartered *Olympic* for service as a troop transport. *Olympic* was in Liverpool for only nine days, commenced her first transatlantic voyage since the war had started, and arrived in Halifax in 28 March. Plans were for *Olympic* to steam to Britain in a convoy, but Captain Hayes expressed concerns that it would make a superb target for U-boats among the small and slow cargo steamers and insisted on leaving the convoy at full speed in order to minimise the U-boat threat.

In 1917, *Olympic* was painted in a dazzle camouflage scheme and was fitted with 6-in guns. After the United States entered the war, *Olympic* ferried thousands of US troops to Britain and while undertaking this role, she actually rammed and sank an enemy U-boat. Loaded with troops, she was steaming towards Britain when in the early morning of 12 May 1918 her look-out spotted a surfaced U-boat close ahead. As *Olympic* was steaming eastbound the lookout could make out the U-boat with the dawn behind it. However, the officers on the conning tower of the U-boat could not see *Olympic* in the pitch-black sky behind it. Captain Hayes gave the order for full speed ahead, straight for the U-boat, which was in a frenzy trying to dive quickly to escape after the lookouts had finally spotted *Olympic*. The 46,000-ton *Olympic* sliced through *U-103* just aft of her conning tower. Thirty-one survivors were later picked up by the USS *Davis*. An ocean liner had sunk an enemy U-boat! This was unique in the whole history of the war. Captain Hayes was awarded the Distinguished Conduct Medal and *Olympic*'s lookout received the Distinguished Service Cross as well as £20 from White Star Line for saving its great liner.

OLYMPIC'S POST-WAR SERVICE

Hostilities ended on 8 November 1918. *Olympic* was in New York at the armistice and a few days later left to cross the Atlantic without a black-out – the first in four years. Her task was now to ferry thousands of troops back to Canada and the United States. In August 1919, *Olympic* returned to Harland & Wolff to be refitted as a passenger liner. During this work, while in dry-dock, a large crack was found in the

Olympic in her prime. In the 1920s she was a firm favourite of ocean travellers. These were her happiest days.

shell plating below the waterline. Nobody knew what had caused this. The double hull prevented the ship from sinking. Captain Hayes suggested that his ship had been torpedoed and that the torpedo failed to explode.

The biggest alteration that took place during this refit was the conversion from coal burning to oil burning. Oil was more expensive than coal, but this measure would reduce the fuelling time from days to hours. In addition, the number of engine-room crew was reduced from 350 to 60.

However, White Star Line needed a companion for *Olympic* to continue its weekly service. Most British shipping companies were to benefit from the availability of ships taken as prizes from Germany. Cunard received some to partially replace ships it had lost in the war. White Star Line received Hamburg Amerika's *Bismarck*, which was still under construction, as well as Norddeutscher Lloyd's *Columbus*. *Bismarck* became *Majestic* and *Columbus* took on the new name *Homeric*. The service operated by

these three ships began in 1922 and lasted until 1930, when the Great Depression reduced demand.

The 1920s were the best years for *Olympic*. She became a firm favourite of ocean travellers and earned herself the nickname 'Old Reliable'. However, in 1934 she rammed and sank the Nantucket light-ship in thick fog. Seven of the lightship's crew perished. Shortly afterwards, the British government forced the merger of White Star Line interests and Cunard Steam Ship Co Ltd. Cunard White Star Ltd started sorting out surplus tonnage that consisted mainly of old White Star liners, including *Olympic*. In 1935, she was sold to be scrapped at Jarrow and provided much-needed work for the area. In September 1937, the remains of *Olympic*, which were by then down to the waterline, were towed to T W Ward's yard at Inverkeithing for final demolition.

Thus ended Lord Pirrie's and J Bruce Ismay's dream of a trio of large Atlantic liners, two of which never completed a commercial voyage.

Below: Falling Star. After the merging of Cunard and the White Star Line, Cunard White Star started to weed out obsolete ships, amongst them the *Olympic*. Lying here in Southampton, the altered arrangement of windows can be seen on B-deck after staterooms had been added.

Model Products

The ocean-liner aficionado is not as well served by the plastic model industry as is the battleship enthusiast, let alone the war-bird fan. Good kits of *Bismarck* and *Tirpitz*, for example, come out regularly from various manufacturers in the Far East in such a quality that one can only drool over the contents. Studying the parts of an unbuilt, well-produced plastic model kit can be just as entertaining as reading a good book. Sadly for liner modellers, there are probably as many *Bismarck* kits around as all kits of ocean liners put together. Models of the latter fall into two categories – plastic models from which a true masterpiece can be built, even if it requires a lot of work; and kits whose quality makes them no more than toys (these are omitted).

In 1975, Entex stunned the plastic modelling world with the release of its 1/350-scale *Titanic*. It was the first plastic model kit of *Titanic* to be released and to this day it still remains among the best, despite

its age. It is marketed today by Minicraft and has undergone a substantial update to rectify mistakes and to clean up the moulds.

The first plastic model kit of the *Titanic* was released in 1975 by Entex in 1/350 scale. This model is still available today from Minicraft. The moulds have been refurbished since.

MINICRAFT (FORMERLY ENTEX) — 1/350 Scale

Well over 450 parts moulded in black, tan, white, brown, clear polystyrene and 'gold-plated' plastic are supplied. The most impressive is the one-piece hull that features rather heavy shell plating detail.

Eight sprues contain the mass of parts, while the larger items such as decks are all individually packed in seperate plastic bags. Railings and ladders are also included, but due to the moulding process these are a little on the heavy side and should be replaced with photo-etched items. However, models built carefully straight from the box can also look very impressive. According to the instructions, some vents face in the wrong direction and as a result the modeller will need to check these with *Titanic* photographs. Poor fit of parts, no location pips, over-excessive detail, and sometimes warped decks, make this a kit for the experienced. The 'Modelmakers' Showcase' explains how some real masterpieces can be made from this kit. It is still by far the best plastic model kit available of the great liner.

The Minicraft kit as available today.

The Entex kit that was available from Minicraft in the 1990s.

REVELL   1/570 Scale

■ With its 1976 release, Revell was the second company to kit the famous liner. Generally aimed at the younger modeller, a different market to the offering from Entex/Minicraft, this kit is a rather modest approach, albeit one with an accurate outline. No doubt the Entex version helped Revell design its kit. In an effort to make its kit as complete as possible, Revell has included the deck railing on each deck as solid walls. To remove these would be a serious undertaking in itself and the modeller should brace himself for some substantial plastic surgery. However, the model by Christopher Martinez shows that it can be done! Shrouds and funnel ladders are moulded in plastic and consequently are very heavy and should be replaced. This is not a bad kit. It is ideal to introduce a younger modeller to plastic model ships and for those seeking the real challenge it can be transformed into a true masterpiece after a lot of work because the outline of the ship is very accurate.

The Revell kit is available today in an enormous box and includes glue and paint.

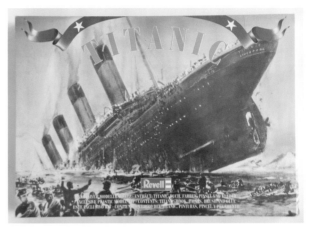

Revell followed hot on the heels of Entex in 1977 with the release of their 1/570 scale kit. It is still available today.

REVELL   1/400 Scale

■ Released in the late 1990s, one could have wished for a better product. Computer-aided technology had long since become standard in model kit production when this kit was released and it marked a vast improvement in the overall quality of kits of the day. However, not with this kit. Nine sprues and two separate hull halves are moulded in white. In an effort to include yet again everything, railings are included (in some cases moulded to the deckhouse walls and which makes removal easier), but these are all a little on the heavy side. A lot of detail, such as bench seats (some in the wrong place) and electric winches, is moulded on to the decks. The funnels are too circular when viewed from above. The same applies to this kit that applies to Revell's smaller kit. With a lot of work this can be turned into a fine model because the basic outline is fairly correct.

ACADEMY

This kit stands out as one of the finest moulded kits of *Titanic*. Released in 1998, the technology was certainly in place to produce better kits than those from the 1970s. It is very crisply moulded in four colours and also includes a clear and 'gold-plated' sprue. The break-down of parts shows clever tooling and makes for strong joints on the completed model. However, unfortunately Academy did not do its home-work. A lot of new information had come to light between the Entex model of the mid-1970s and the ·Academy version some twenty-three years later. Most of it has not been included in this kit – on the contrary, Academy made the same mistakes that Entex did in 1975. Academy even excluded the two Engelhardt collapsible lifeboats on the boat deck!

The basic outline is not good! Shell plating on the hull overlaps towards the bow; on *Titanic* it was towards the stern, as on most ships. The shell plating pattern has no resemblance of that of the real ship.

Very recently, Academy re-released this

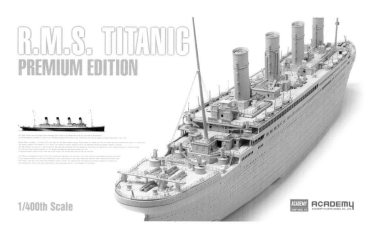

kit with a huge amount of photo-etched pieces for railings, windows and many other details. The striking box top shows this model completely painted in light grey with the unpainted brass photo-etched bits attached. It is quite a sight! This set certainly upgrades the kit enormously, but it does not rectify the faults. Nonetheless, a stunning model can be built from this kit.

Academy's *Titanic* in its limited edition form. 1500 units were released.

AIRFIX

This model, too, will be ideal for starting a child in plastic modelling, and even more so when there is a personal interest in the ship. It is not too expensive and it is easy to build. It is cleanly moulded and detail is excellent for a kit of this size.

The 1/700 model of *Titanic* by Airfix.

HAHN/REED/DAVIES-GARNER

This is described in the 'Model Detail Accessories' section.

The Mantua 1/200 plank-on-frame kit and its detailed instruction manual. See Rinie Egas' model from this kit on page 28.

Model Detail Accessories

In recent years, several enthusiasts have released photo-etched sets to upgrade kits – even in the smallest scales.

Gold Medal Models

The GMM 1/350 figure set, including the ship's orchestra and captain.

MERCHANT SHIP SETS

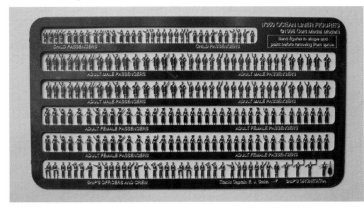

1/700 scale

Starting with 1/700 scale, Gold Medal Models (www.goldmm.com) has released its Merchant Ship Set, which includes ladders, railings, lifeboat pulleys, shrouds (for the *Olympic* class liners and *Mauretania/Lusitania*), crane hooks and lifebelts. The detail is amazing, but, needless to say, the parts are very delicate. The railings are not made to fit; it is up for the modeller to trim these accordingly. Of course these will be useful for any other ocean liner in that scale.

1/600 and 1/400 scale

Gold Medal has also released the same set in 1/600 and 1/400 scale. Due to the popularity of the 1/350 Minicraft kit, the majority of items are available in that scale.

1/350 scale

The 1/350 Merchant Ship Set is not a scaled-up copy of its smaller sets. In this set the railings are made to fit the 1/350 kits of *Lusitania* and *Titanic*.

It includes railings, ladders, stairs, lifeboat pulleys, shrouds, crane hooks and lifebelts. There are enough parts for one ship but several parts will be left over after completion.

The GMM 1/350 lifeboat davits set.

OCEAN LINER FIGURE SET

For those would like to add a little life to their models, this set comprises over 200 figures, including the captain and the ships' orchestra, passengers, children and crew members.

TITANIC/LUSITANIA SET

This includes Marconi wire spreaders, cargo booms and support racks, compass tower struts, ship's wheel, specially designed railings for cargo crane bases, docking bridge supports, first class deckchairs and lifeboat safety lines.

Tom's Modelworks

Tom's Modelworks (www.tomsmodelworks. com) has produced six brass photo-etched frets in 1/350 scale:

***Titanic* Railings No 3511:** Consists of 3-, 4- and 5-bar railings made to fit. It also includes stairs and shrouds (*Titanic* only).

Deckchairs No 3533: a small fret with forty deckchairs.

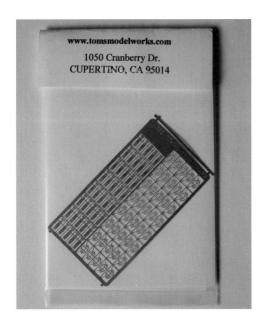

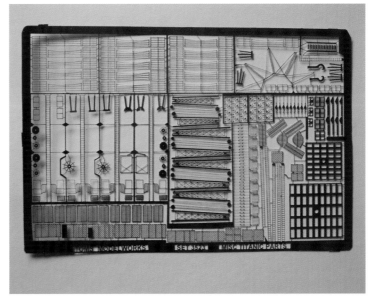

***Titanic* Detail set No 3523:** Includes both grand staircase dome covers to fit the kit walls, crew skylights, crane jibs, hooks, supports and railings for operators' platforms, funnel ladders and platforms, fiddley gratings, stokehold vents wire meshes, lifeboat gripes, etc.

***Titanic* Benches No 3522:** Small fret consisting of forty-eight bench seats.

***Titanic* Windows No 3521:** Consists of windows for the entire ship, including verandah cafe sliding doors, and engine room skylight covers.

Boat Davits and Miscellaneous Details No 3551: Complete set of davits and other details, such as tie-down ropes, grab-ropes, pulleys, leadsman's platform and coaling outriggers.

Above left: Tom's Modelworks' 1/350 deckchairs

Above: Tom's Modelworks' 1/350 scale Misc. Titanic parts set 3523.

Ocean Liner Models

Tom Nicolai of Ocean Liner Models (www.oceanlinermodels.com) produced a 1/350 *Olympic* and *Britannic* conversion set. Unfortunatly, at the moment he does not offer these for sale but he can be contacted via his website. The conversion sets were very well done and are still much in demand.

Robert Hahn

1/144t scale resin funnel distributed by Robert Hahn. The funnels have the correct rivet pattern.

1/144 SCALE

Through Robert Hahn's website (www.Titanic-Plan.de), a 1/144-scale semi-kit is available. The products for this come from various sources, including the author. This semi-kit should only be approached by experienced modellers.

Dan Reed from the United States produces the hull and several resin fittings. This 1.86-metre fibreglass hull is moulded in one piece and has complete shell plating, portholes, gangway ports, etc, but there are no rivets. Surplus material needs to be removed along the top edge of the hull and some blemishes resulting from the moulding process need to be cleaned up.

The resin set consists of all four funnels, all cowl and Sirocco vents, lifeboats and cranes (sans jibs – these are in the photo-etched set).

All of the items are well moulded but lack some detail. The Sirocco vents are moulded in one piece and are a little crude. However, the complete set serves as a superb basis for the super-detailer. The funnels are superb and have the correct rivet pattern. The boats are solid and all 30-ft lifeboats are covered; the two emergency cutters are open but need some detail added. I am not completely happy with the outline of the boats.

Robert Hahn now also offers a cnc-milled deckhouse and superstructure set. Produced in very thick white styrene, the

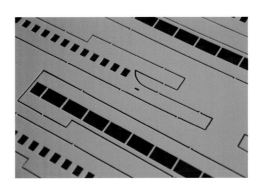

Robert Hahn Promenade deck hull screens.

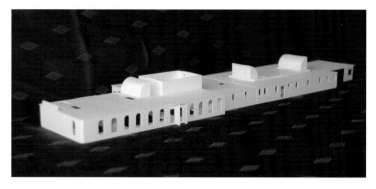

Above: Robert Hahn officers' quarters and gymnasium.

Above right: Robert Hahn 1/144 scale PE-detail set.

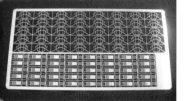

Above: Robert Hahn 1/144 deckchairs.

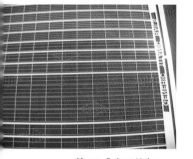

Above: Robert Hahn 1/144 scale railings. Note that the thicker strips are not the wooden handrails but the kicking-strips.

Right: Robert Hahn 1/144 fairlead and bollard base-plate set.

Far right: Robert Hahn 1/144th scale bench-seats.

Below: Robert Hahn 1/144 scale davits in detail.

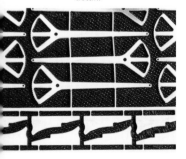

quality is superb. As far as I am concerned, the gymnasium-style windows are grossly over scale and the second class smoke room windows are wrong.

The whole set consists of deckhouses and superstructure for the whole ship as well as A-deck hull sides will be added in the future.

The set comes complete with styrene windows, to which the etched frames are to be added.

The photo-etched set consists of several frets:

Frets A+B: All window frames, doors, both grand staircase skylight covers, funnel ladders and mast ladders, 200 Utleys swivel portholes, all skylights, wire mesh for vent shafts, funnel platforms and crane platforms, all stairs and ladders, propeller bosses.

Fret C: Crane jibs, shrouds, lifeboat davits, wire mesh for Sirocco vents, compass platform, crow's nest, lifeboat grab ropes, forecastle breakwater, etc.

Fret D: Davit arms, lifeboat chocks, struts for crane jibs, fourth funnel cover, steampipe cover on forecastle deck, gangway ports for hull sides.

All the above frets were produced by Robert Hahn. This is no doubt a very ambitious

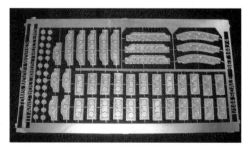

set, which will keep the serious modeller very busy for a long while.

The following frets are also available via www.Titanic-Plan.de and were produced by Tom's Modelworks:

Bench seat set: Forty-eight bench seats, including a template for folding these to the correct shape. There are two frets. Recent research has shown that there were at least two different lengths for the bench seats. The set offered here gives one length for all benches.

Deckchair set: Forty deckchairs.

Railings and shrouds: Somewhat of a disappointment because the railings are too thin and lack the removable rails to give access to the fairleads on the forecastle and poop deck. Jörg Graffe has produced an alternative set that should be available through the author by the time this work has been published. However, the majority of modelmakers that have used Tom's Modelworks railing set might be perfectly happy with it.

Fairlead and bollard foundation kit: These can be made from thin sheet styrene with no problems at all. In addition, the etched fairlead foundations have the wrong shape.

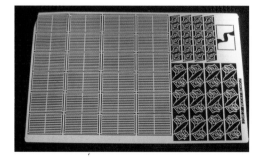

Davies-Garner

Due to the missing rivets on the 1/144-scale hull, the author has produced a photo-etched shell plating set. This consists of three large A3-size frets and one small A4 size. A further small set has been produced and this features lifeboat blocks and railings, handrail brackets, propeller blades and other items. To prevent warping, these sheets are

etched in silver.

The author has also released a 1/144-scale resin forecastle, poop and well deck set. It consists of more than 200 items to fully detail these decks. The author can be contacted at PANDavies@aol.com

Both 1/144-scale models shown in 'Modelmakers' Showcase' were built using these items.

Modelmakers' Showcase

TITANIC 1/144 scale

By JÖRG GRAFFE

This exceptional model was built using the Hahn/Reed/Davies-Garner semi-kit.

Materials:

– *Titanic* semi-kit, Robert Hahn/Daniel Reed
– set of etched parts, Robert Hahn
– lifeboat railings, resin parts (bollards, capstans etc), Peter Davies-Garner
– etched railings, benches, davit rigging, Jörg Graffe
– decals, signs, flags, Jörg Graffe
– various colours by Revell and Humbrol
– polystyrene strips and sheets
– acrylic glass blocks
– maple veneer

References:

– *RMS Titanic: A Modelmaker's Manual*, Peter Davies-Garner
– Hahn's *Titanic* Plans

– *Titanic – The Ship Magnificent*, Vols I & II, Beveridge *et al.*
– *Titanic and her sisters Olympic and Britannic*, McCluskie *et al.*
– TRMA, Titanic Research and Modeling Association, titanic-model.com
– various other books and web pages

Additional photos of the model, as well as additional information and sources of supply can be found online at:

http://www.joerg.graffe.de
Contact: joerg@graffe.de

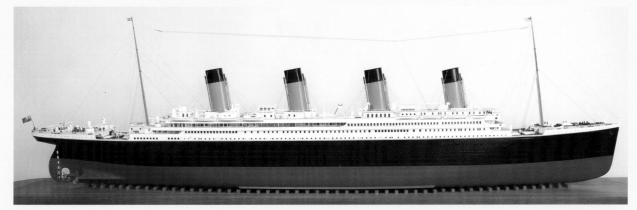

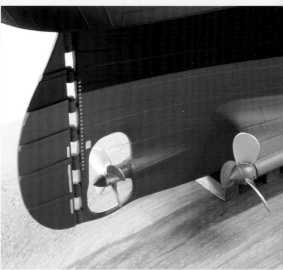

TITANIC 1/144 scale

By MORTEN JENSEN

This model is what is called a semi-kit, which means that a few parts are available, but much of the model has to be made from scratch. The hull, funnels, lifeboats, vents and some deck pieces are resin parts that are provided by Daniel Reed. Many brass parts, made by Robert Hahn and Tom's Modelworks, are also available. The plans I mostly used for this were 1/144 scale model plans, but the general arrangement plans by Bruce Beveridge were used from time to time.

Hull: The hull is made of fibreglass and was part of the kit. The detailing of the hull is very good and I did not do very much to the hull itself. All portholes were drilled out and the square windows were drilled out and cleaned in the edges by use of a Dremel and a file. The propeller bosses are of styrene with a brass tube inside for the propeller shafts, so they do not need any alteration if one decides to do an RC model. The bosses were glued to the fibreglass hull, and putty was used to fill all the gaps to make one smooth surface.

Details that I added to the hull were the intakes for the engines, outtakes from the condensers, mooring ports, bilge keels and the keel plate. All of these details can be found in the plans. As the rudder post is not complete in the fibreglass hull, the post needs to be built from scratch. This was done by using the plans and sheet styrene. When this was done, the surface was puttied and sanded and the hinges for the rudder were added. The rudder is also a part of the hull kit and is made of resin.

Superstructure, bulkheads and deckhouses: All of the superstructure, bulkheads and deckhouses were made of sheet styrene in different thicknesses – mostly 0.10 in and 0.20 in. Most of the corners, windows, portholes and details were measured directly from the 1/144 scale plans. When cut to shape, detailed parts such as window frames and hand railings were added before the bulkheads were sprayed. The window frames are part of the brass set, and the railings are made from 0.20-in styrene rod. I found that painting these details after they were glued to the bulkhead and sprayed was easier and gave a better result. Adding railings and such after spraying is also possible, but one has to beware of glue spillage in the wrong places because some types of glue will dissolve the paint and leave a mess. After painting, the details were sharp and crisp.

All of the bulkheads and deckhouses were stiffened on the back with thicker styrene. This was painted black on one side so one can not look through the model. The lines for the bulkheads were drawn on the deck, and the bulkheads were placed where they should be and glued from behind so no spilling would be visible at all.

Decks: All of the decks were made of 1-mm sheet styrene, and the wooden decks were covered with 0.6-mm wooden veneer. I chose beech because this is light in colour and is almost without grain. The veneer was cut into 1-mm wide strips and laid over the styrene. After the glue had set, the veneer was sanded so that the decks were

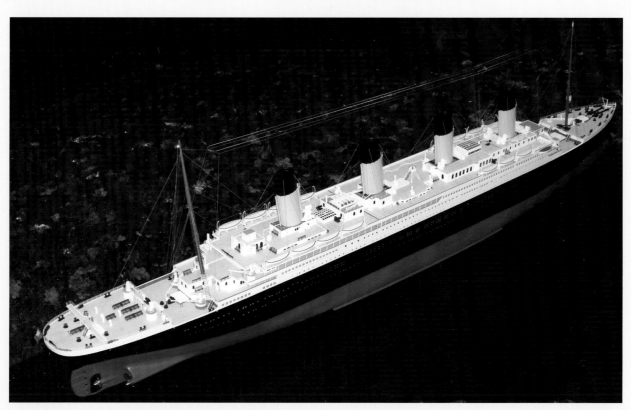

perfectly smooth. This process took some time, but the result was worth the work because the appearance is far better than if plastic decks were used. The decks not covered with wood were of 0.50-mm styrene and strengthened on the underside. All of the decks were glued on top of the bulkheads, and strips of 0.25-mm styrene were glued around to hide and simulate the edges.

Funnels: The funnels are part of the semi-kit and are very well detailed. All rivets are included, and not much is needed to do to the funnels except cleaning and removing the flash. The ladders, platform and platform railings are included in the brass set. All piping and whistles were made from styrene.

Fittings: All of the vents for the model were part of the resin kit provided by Daniel Reed. Some of these vents needed alterations, and details such as gratings were available from the brass set.

The lifeboats were also resin parts, and the grab-lines were in the brass set. These were spray painted, and the White Star Line flags were painted on by hand because I did not have decals for these. The davits are all brass, and are provided in the brass set. These took some time to assemble, but look good when finished. Ropes and tackles were made from styrene rod and stretched sprue from other kits.

The cranes are part resin pieces and partly brass. The crane bases and the main part of the crane are made of resin, and the crane arm and ladders are brass. Parts such as the handles are made from styrene rod.

Much of the forecastle, poop and well

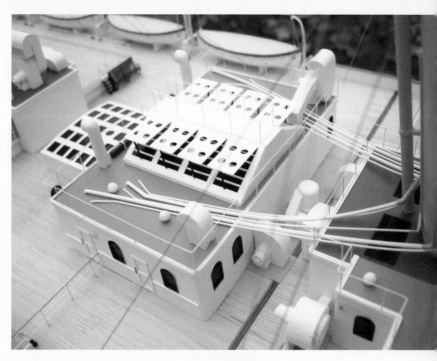

deck details are part of the resin kit. These included bollards, capstans, fairleads, steam winches, electric winches, cargo hatches, anchor winches, kedge and stream anchors, hawse reels, cowl vents and rollers. Because so much is available, this part of the detailing was completed quickly. The detail and accuracy on these parts are really good.

Masts and rigging: It was hard to find any masts ready to add to the model and I had to make my own. I was thinking about turning these from box wood, but found another method. I used wooden paint-brushes. These had the perfect coning for the masts, so did not need much work. But because they were too short, I had to cut the tip of one and attach it to the end of another. When set, I fastened the entire mast in an electric drill and held it down on sandpaper while running the drill. That way the tips of the masts were perfectly sanded to shape. Details such as bands around the cargo derrick, masts and lanterns were made from styrene. The masts were then tapered and added to the model. The crow's nest is part of the brass set and was detailed additionally using styrene pieces. To get the correct thickness for the rigging, I used several types of thread. Most of the rigging, such as mast stays, Marconi wires and funnels stays, are made from fishing lines in different sizes. Other rigging was made from nylon thread. As all of these

threads are produced of clear materials, these were painted after they were stretched on the model.

Name, flags and signs: The name and port of registry are water decals produced by a friend. Because printing yellow on water decals can be very tricky, I had these printed with the letters left clear and the surrounding area black. I then painted in yellow the area where these were to be located. When the decals were placed over them, the yellow would shine through the clear letters in the decals. The result was perfect. It was the same person that printed the different signs around the models for me after I had designed them myself. These were made as stickers and simply stuck on the railings. The flags were hand painted by me on aluminium foil. This took some time, but was worth the effort. After the flags were fastened to the model, the foil could be gently bent into better shape to make them look more realistic.

MANTUA *TITANIC* 1/200 scale

By RINIE EGAS

'... the musicians kept playing while the ship was sinking ...'. This always made the biggest impression on me when I heard *Titanic*'s story as a child. Ever since reading that, I have been interested in the world's most famous ship. So when I was looking for a new model kit, two years ago, *Titanic* was high on the list. I had built a few small plastic and wooden ship model kits and was looking for a more challenging project to build a large wooden ship model. I searched the Internet and stumbled upon the Mantua kit. It looked interesting because of its size, good quality and detailed instructions. In January 2009, I bought the kit and the building journey began.

Hull: The Mantua kit comes in four boxes: two boxes containing the parts for the hull and the deck fittings and two boxes containing the superstructure parts and detailed fittings. There is a fifth box containing a motor and electronic equipment to create a radio control version of the model. I skipped this part and built a static version. I could not bear the idea of putting the model in the water after years of work.

The project started with building the hull. The 1.35-m long hull is constructed in the plank on frame method. This was a first for me, but I was comforted by the fact that I could finish the hull with primer and paint after the planking was done.

Knowing that the hull can make or break a model, I worked slowly and precisely. The first step was to attach the twenty-four frames to the keel. I checked and double-checked that all of the frames were nicely straight and aligned. Once the frames were in position, the planks could be attached. Adding layer after layer of planks to the frames slowly gave the ship the familiar *Titanic* shape. During the build I noticed that the stern of the model was too wide. I had to narrow down the stern frames quite a bit to prevent a 'fat bottomed' *Titanic*.

When all of the planks were in place, the finishing could begin. I followed the process of sanding the hull, adding a thin layer of primer and sanding it again. Repeating this process a few times resulted in a nicely smoothed hull. In August 2009, I finished the hull by attaching the hull plates, which gives the hull a riveted steel look and brings out details such as portholes and doors.

Superstructure: Having finished the hull, I continued with the decks. All decks were planked with 2-mm wide wooden strips. The kit contains nice laser-etched plywood sheets to construct the cabins of the upper decks. These easily came together and only needed a few layers of paint. Construction of the funnels was more complicated. Like almost all parts of the kit, the funnels are made of wood. The funnels consist of a wooden frame around which a wooden plywood plank needs to be wrapped. It took a lot of warm water and patience to get the planks nicely into shape.

Finishing the model: In August 2010, the main structural work was done and now I could start with the detailed fittings: davits, lifeboats, railings, ladders, stairs, rigging, and so on.

Although the kit has many fittings, I was not satisfied with the detail of some of the parts. Since they are made of wood, some were just too coarse for the 1/200 scale. To

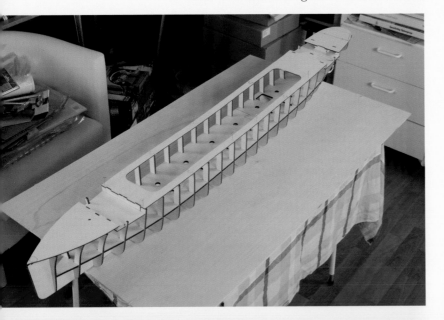

solve this I bought Tom's Modelworks' after-market photo-etched (PE) set. This 1/196 scale PE set contains highly detailed parts that I used to replace the kit's wooden railings, stairs and ladders. Although there is a small difference in scale, most parts fit nicely.

Working on the fittings is a real joy. Every new detail brings the model more to life. And for every part it's a challenging puzzle to get it in the right shape, colour and position. Since the beginning of this project, I have been keeping a building log on a number of Internet modelling forums.[1] This proves to be a great source of information, because many fellow model builders give me useful advice and answer the many questions I have. Next to that I get much information and inspiration from two books: *RMS Titanic – A Modelmaker's*

Manual[2] and *Titanic: The Ship Magnificent*.[3] At the time of writing (March 2011), I estimate that the model will be completed within six months. I want to at least be finished before the centenary of *Titanic*'s maiden voyage, 10 April 2012.

Notes
[1] Internet modelling build forums on which I keep a building log: www.model-shipworld.com, www.titanic-model.com, www.modelships-beagle.eu/smf, www.modelbouw1.be, www.model-brouwers.nl
[2] Peter Davies-Garner, *RMS Titanic – A Modelmaker's Manual*.
[3] Bruce Beveridge, Scott Andrews, Steve Hall and Daniel Klistorner, *Titanic: The Ship Magnificent: Volume 1: Design and Construction*.

Kit Review: Mantua assembled a good quality kit. The kit has excellent building instructions that consist of photo booklets showing and describing all building steps. The quality of the wood is good and most parts fit without too much need for modifications. The shape of the hull frames could be improved. The frames require significant modifications to get the stern narrowed down. The wooden railings, ladders and stairs are very coarse. I replaced them with a PE set. General impression: very good (4/5); instructions: excellent (5/5); wood quality: good (3/5); detailing of fittings: good (3/5).

TITANIC WRECK 1/144 scale

By MORTEN JENSEN

This was the first 1/144-scale model that I ever built, and was first thought to be some sort of testing model before I started a 1/144 *Titanic*. As I worked and the model gradually turned out to look like something, I soon figured out that working with the 1/144 scale was a great experience. This resembles the wreck as it appeared when it was explored by Ballard in 1986.

This model started as 4-mm plywood. The frames were cut out using the 1/144 *Titanic* model plans as a guide. After assembly of all of the frames, the skeleton was cut and then reassembled at an angle to resemble the way that *Titanic* settled after she hit the ocean floor. From there, I started adding the shell plating. At this time Peter Davies-Garner was offering a 1/144-scale brass set with some of the plating for the ship. As this set included highly detailed screens for B, C and D decks, it was simple to cut and bend these pieces to shape. The rest of the shell plating was built of sheet styrene, except for the buckled areas, such as under the well deck and on and around the break-up area, where the shell plating was made of latex rubber. I first made a hull side on a separate sheet of styrene in 1/144 scale. I then did a plaster mould of this and covered the mould with many thin layers of latex rubber applied with a paintbrush. When thick enough to keep the detailing of the hull, the latex was removed from the mould and I then had a copy of the shell plating. The latex was

glued on one end at first so it was easier to bend. One problem with the latex is that it can be tricky to cut into shape, but in time I got it right. When added to the model, it was then stiffened on the back to make it less fragile. For the decks, I used 1-mm sheet styrene.

With the decks and all shell plating added, both straight and bent, the basic hull was done up to B-deck. But as the grand staircase would be an open hole into the model and several of the doors in the hull would be left open, a lot of work had to be done inside the model before adding more decks. Also, the cargo hatches were gone so the inside of these areas had to be

detailed. The grand staircase would require most of the work as I built each deck following the plans. Starting on E-deck, there would be much debris and this deck is therefore hard to see on the model. On D-deck, the remains of the steel structure for the once so elegant staircase is still there. The D-deck Reception Room spans the entire width of the ship, and as a result this required much work with all the bulkheads, columns, debris and other detailing. Also, the entrances were detailed from the plans. The doors leading to the reception room even have the wrought iron panels in them. These doors are also left open, so one can see through the entire model and also see much of the framing from the stairs in the middle. The remaining decks would be easier to build because they were smaller and needed less work, but followed the plans.

It was time to build up the rest of the structure. The A-deck was added together with the bulkheads. As some of the windows still have framing, I used the window frames from the 1/144 brass set for the 1/144 semi-kit. Before the boat deck was added, all deck beams, pipes, rusticles and rust colour were added before the deck was glued in place. This would have been too difficult to accomplish after the deck was fitted. The A-deck also had to be painted and 'rusted' before the boat deck was added. With A-deck completed and the boat deck added, the remaining bulkheads for the deckhouses could be added. This was mostly a straightforward process, because I had the plans. Where any bulkheads were either bent or damaged so one could see the inside, all beams and girders were added. As the funnels are all gone, the casings left two big holes into the ship and which also needed attention. The holes in the model go about half way down in the structure and I have added as much detail and debris inside and around them as I could. All of this was of course done with the aid of photographs of the real wreck. The twisted remains of the funnels and surrounding parts are made from

aluminium foil, so I could easily bend and shape the parts correctly. The boilers at the break-up area were all made from sheet styrene and added before the collapsed decks were in place. These decks are made from both styrene and cardboard. I have never used cardboard for anything on my models but for the warped decks the cardboard worked perfectly. Everything would be covered with rusticles and painted later.

Now that the ship itself was together and its biggest features were in place, the detailing could begin. For the cranes, bollards, and some other forecastle fittings I used the 1/144 resin detail set. For the railings I used the 1/144 brass railings from Tom's Modelworks. As most of the railings are either gone or heavily twisted, I spent

some time studying photographs in order to get the smallest pieces of railing bent correctly. In some places only a single stanchion remains from a railing, such as on the top of the grand staircase foyer. All vents were also built from styrene and 'damaged' correctly. The mast is made from a wooden paintbrush because this had the perfect shape and size. The crow's nest is made from the same foil as that around the funnel casings because this had to be distorted quite heavily. Styrene tends to bend itself back to the original shape, so foil worked much better here. The davits and the boat chocks are PE brass parts also from Tom's

Modelworks. Most of the rigging is gone on the wreck, but a few pieces remain, such as on the forecastle and around the end of the mast in the area near the navigating bridge. Attention was paid to ensure that these pieces of rigging hanging or lying on the model are just as on the real wreck. Any other small details not mentioned were usually made from styrene pieces.

With the model done, it was ready for the seabed and painting. The model was placed on a wooden frame and the seabed was built up around it with Styrofoam plates. For the biggest rusticles on the model I used regular acryl. I used a toothpick and simply dipped the acryl on the required area and then pulled the acryl so it formed a rusticle. This was done to most sharp edges around the model, such as the overhang from the A-deck, vents, railings, mast, etc. When this was finished and dried, I used a special decor spray called 'fleck spray' and covered the entire model – sometimes several layers. This leaves a very rough and uneven surface when dried, so it worked nicely to simulate the smaller rusticles and corrosion. Sand was now added to the ocean floor. When this was done, the entire model was painted in the 1912 colours with the red bottom, black hull and white superstructure. When I airbrushed the entire model in several rust colours the 'original' paint could still barely be seen under everything. Upon completion, one can see that it is slightly lighter in colour on the top than on the original black part of the hull.

MINICRAFT *TITANIC* 1/350 scale   By MORTEN JENSEN

It was my intention to make this model of a better standard than provided in the kit. The additional detailing to the hull was made by using styrene pieces. All portholes were drilled out and hawse pipes were also added. The decks for the model are the decks provided in the kit with 0.6-mm beech wooden veneer added on top. Some decking does not have any wooden covering, and these were made from sheet styrene. Parts such as the fairleads on the poop deck and the forecastle were first removed and rebuilt on top of the veneer.

The bulkheads are also from the kit and were altered in a few places to make the configuration correct. This also applied to the doors and windows because they were not entirely accurate. Window frames are provided in the brass set from Tom's Modelworks (TMW). These were painted and added to the bulkheads.

With the hull, decking and bulkheads in place, the detailing could start. Almost all of the vents were either altered or rebuilt, in styrene, to give the correct appearance. The funnels in the kit have a nice overall shape, but because the detailing is too rough, the bands were removed and replaced with thinner bands made of styrene. Funnel ladders and railings are available in the brass detail kit from TMW. The cranes are a combination of the kit pieces, TMW brass parts and a few scratch-built parts. The

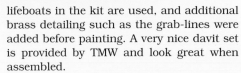

lifeboats in the kit are used, and additional brass detailing such as the grab-lines were added before painting. A very nice davit set is provided by TMW and look great when assembled.

Other parts such as the benches, all railings, ratlines, compass tower, stairs and ladders, are all parts from different brass sets from TMW. With these parts, it is all about preparation and making sure they will fit perfectly on the model, because most of the parts, especially the railings, need much bending. All of these brass parts were painted before being added to the model. All rigging on the model is done by nylon thread and this was painted after it was added. The nylon thread is clear and it would look unrealistic if not painted.

This 1/350 model is in my opinion the best model to resemble a 'shelf-size' model of *Titanic*. It can either be built from 'out of the box' and it will still be a nice looking model that is also fun to build, or it can be improved to better resemble the great ship.

OLYMPIC 1/350 scale

By BRIAN DISNEY

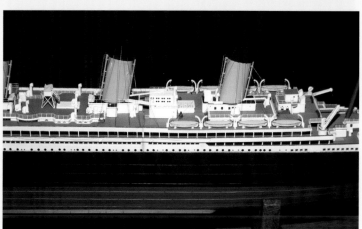

Since no kit of *Olympic* exists, if a modeller wishes to create that ship it would have to be done from scratch. Luckily, when working on my Southampton diorama, I made the acquaintance of Ray Lepien from the Titanic Historical Society and the Titanic Research and Modeling Association. When I finished the diorama and began my next project, Ray provided me with reference material for my conversion. Bud Hovestadt wrote an article for the June/July 1996 issue of *Scale Ship Modeler* and this dealt with converting Minicraft's 1/350-scale *Titanic* into *Olympic*. His step-by-step instructions were very easy to follow and resulted in a very nice finished product. The major conversions were the opening up of the A-deck (promenade), removing part of the aft end of B-deck, and altering the remaining B-deck windows. The use of the kit plastic one-rail handrails created the B-deck windows and the other two conversions were just scratch-built. Keeping the new stanchions straight and evenly spaced was the biggest concern for the newly opened A-deck. After that, the kit is built mostly the same as a *Titanic* would be and finished with Gold Medal Models

photo-etched brass parts. One thing which I did was add some 'canvas' at several locations. The canvas is simply a single layer of tissue that is stiffened with white glue thinned with water. I put some at the forward part of the forecastle, the railings on the roof of the officers' quarters and on the compass platform. The letters used for the name were dry transfer decals. All of my models are protected by a custom-built base and covered with a Plexiglass top.

OLYMPIC 1/570 scale

By CHRIS MARTINEZ

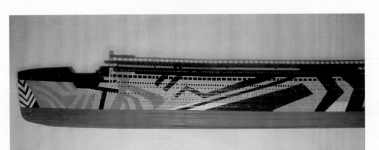

Although this amazing model is not completed, it is one of the few that shows *Olympic* in wartime dazzle camouflage. It is a conversion from the Revell 1/570-scale *Titanic* kit. Here the builder has gone through the trouble of removing the 'solid-wall railings' and has replaced these with photo-etched items. A lot of research has gone into this model as can be seen by the level of detail. It is to be completed as a diorama showing *Olympic* entering New York.

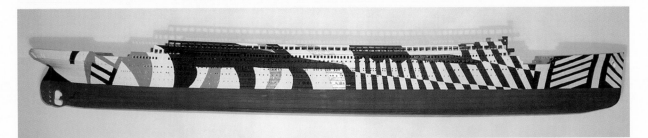

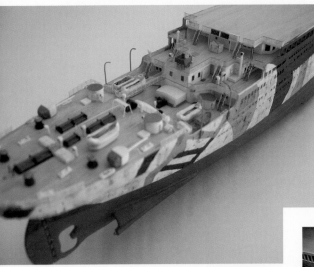

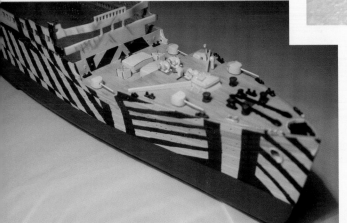

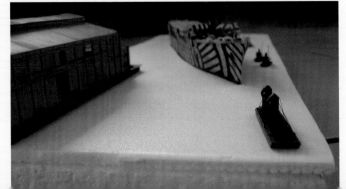

BRITANNIC 1/350 scale

By REMCO HILLEN

The starting point of this model is the Minicraft 1/350-scale *Titanic*. Add-ons include the brass (eg gantry davits and dome covers) and resin (eg motor houses) sets from Tom Nicolai, brass sets from GMM (railings, cargo cranes) and decals from Bruce Beveridge and Duane Fowler (standard *Titanic* windows for the most part) and Tom Nicolai (*Britannic* decals). Various parts of the model are scratch-built, such as the altered A-deck, the covered well deck, the so-called shade deck and various parts of the gantry davits.

It is virtually impossible to build a completely accurate RMS *Britannic* model, Because she never saw service as such. Of course there are various deck plans, but these did not take the First World War into account. It is quite possible that White Star developed different or new ideas for its new liner for its service after the war. This model is therefore based on, among other things, deck plans, photos from the builder's models, photos from HMHS *Britannic* and *Titanic*, and of *Olympic* throughout various stages of her long career. Even wreck pictures have been used! Therefore, this model is an interpretation of various sources. How many lifeboats would she hold? What is that I see on top of the wheelhouse? Is that a blimp in the picture or is it a mushroom vent? Where is the compass tower? And so on.

Forward area: Most visible change in this area is in the forward well deck. Here the Third Class Entrance is situated, a resin part from Tom Nicolai. Various vents have been added or changed, as has been done on the entire model (*Britannic*'s vents differ from *Titanic*'s; almost all vents on the model have been changed, added or moved). The wheelhouse is an interpretation of the rigging plans and *Olympic* photos. With the compass located here on the model, the compass tower in the centre of the ship has been omitted.

Centre: As said, the compass tower has been left off. Other changes are the added childrens' playroom (opposite the gymnasium), large lift gear house on the officers' quarters and a rebuilt tank room. Also interesting, but difficult to spot, are the 'openings' created in the officers' quarters to house parts of the gantry davit driving gear. With the new and large gantry davits installed on RMS *Britannic*, note how clear the railings are of lifeboats. Although not an enhancement of her profile, this was a huge improvement when compared with *Olympic*'s cluttered boat deck after the *Titanic* disaster.

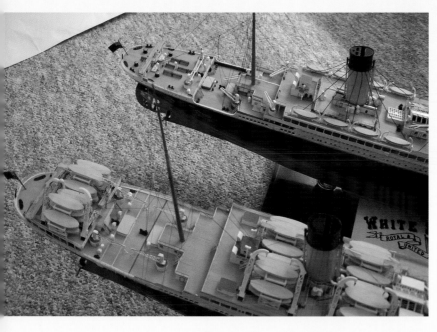

Aft: A lot of scratch building is needed here, such as the roof over the first class smoke room, added dog kennel, extra pieces of the boat deck and A-deck, changed Palm Courts and changed cargo facilities.

Further aft is even more, with the covered aft well deck (now featuring a second class gym), added second class smokeroom on the poop deck and the shade deck (made from sheet styrene with the deck planking scribed into it) covering this.

Gantries: On any RMS *Britannic* model the large gantry davits are eyecatching. With not much about these davits known, at least at the time of building, this was a very time-consuming part of the modelmaking process. The gantries are from the Tom Nicolai kit, with added detailing such as pulleys and ladders. Motor houses and boat racks are also from Tom Nicolai. The driving gears (the black pins coming out of the motor houses), the 'slides' they 'move' in and all of the walkways, are scratch-built. The walkways are constructed from brass railing, blackened, and are supported by other pieces of scratch brass. Various stairs provided access to the boats. Extra lifeboats were created to get to the amount I thought to be correct for RMS *Britannic*. The motor boats near the wheelhouse are 'uncovered' for some extra detailing.

BRITANNIC DIORAMA 1/1200 scale   By MORTEN JENSEN

This model was built to see if I could do something else with the kit than just an ordinary 1/1200-scale *Titanic* model. The kit is the Revell 1/1200 *Titanic* and it was altered to resemble *Britannic* going down. As the ships were very much the same and as this is a very small scale, the alterations took a relatively short time to complete. Some sheet styrene was used to build up new decks and deckhouses. For the new gantry davits, I used the standard Welin davits for a 1/350 Minicraft *Titanic*. The profile of these davits worked perfectly as the new gantry davits. I also added some photo-etched railings, and these are 1/600 railings cut down in height.

The diorama base is a small piece of oak wood covered with aluminium foil, which was first crushed and then smoothed out. That left the foil straight, but with grooves and wrinkles that simulate smaller waves. The hull was cut to shape with a Dremel and placed on the sea, and acryl was used to simulate the larger waves around and out from the ship. I did not add rigging

because I think that could easily cause the model to look cluttered.

I think that this resulted in a nice model and because it required few parts and not too much time to build, it is highly recommended.

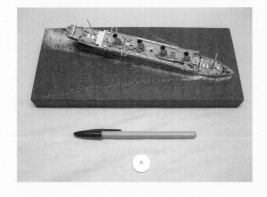

BRITANNIC WRECK 1/350 scale

By WILLIAM BARNEY

When Robert Ballard and his team discovered the wreck of *Titanic* in 1985, I was only six years old and had no knowledge about the ship and its tragic story. I found out that it hit an iceberg and sank on 15 April 1912. It had a hold on me like nothing else. I lived and breathed it. I researched in order to learn more about *Titanic* but then developed an interest in HMHS *Britannic*. What I found fascinating was the rusticles and marine growth that covered both ships' remains. I wanted to model this and began research in order to show the details of how it probably looks down below in those deep waters.

In 2006, I started researching the *Britannic*, but I found very few photos of the wreck. Minimal photos were taken because the British and Greek governments limited viewing of the wreck. This forced me to use my creativity. I would add details using my own interpretation. I discovered the Titanic Research & Modeling Association on the website http//titanic-model.com and contacted Bob Read and Cyril Codus. They provided me with a blueprint. Thanks to Bob and Cyril and their website, I was on my way to creating something that would bring me great joy.

I bought the 1/350-scale *Titanic* to adapt for the *Britannic* wreck, because both hulls are about the same shape. From the lower deck to the boat deck they are from *Titanic*. Everything else I built from scratch.

I raised the aft well deck to the same level as B-deck. I installed the poop deck and added Nos 5 and 6 cargo hatches and put four electric cranes in this area. On the poop deck I added the shade deck. I used a styrene sheet. The docking bridge was put on top of the shade deck. I added two davits on each starboard and port side. Photoshop was used to design the ten gantry davits. I printed these and used superglue to fix them to the cardboard. After drying, I did the same thing on the back. After these were completely dried, I carefully cut the ten gantry davits with a razor and put all four sides on one.

I added gantry davits on the boat deck with the framework where the lifeboats are supported. This was near the first funnel on the starboard side. I added another on the

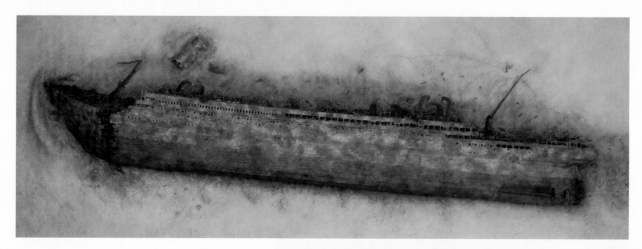

end of the third and fourth funnels on both starboard and port sides. Then I added new sides and a roof to port next to the second funnel and it became the childrens' play-room.

Items by Gold Medal Models and Tom's Modelworks were useful and came from *Titanic* brass detailing products. They do not have any specifically for HMHS *Britannic*, so I had to get some that would fit. I added rail-ings, windows, ladders, davits, stairs, gates and more to make it very detailed.

On the fore well deck, I cut off the parts of the ship to make it depict the damage as it looked when it sank and settled on the bottom of the ocean. I used a candle to soften the plastic in order to get it to bend. I then placed it on the 42 x 20-in wooden board. The board acted as the seabed that became *Britannic*'s resting place. The twists and bends of the decks in the ship are created by the use of pieces of plastic. I wanted the wheelhouse and mortuary to look creepy, so I used tiny plastic styrene strips on the sides and roof. I also used a razor to cut it so it resembled rotting wood.

I almost lost my mind when I was working on the weathering of the *Britannic* wreck, but I was really pleased when it turned out exactly as I envisaged! It shows how the marine growth has taken over most of the wreck. I thought that if I did not add those details, I would not be making it truly authentic. I had the idea to replicate it so it looked like the 1940–50s era, during the war. I used around 50 per cent of the orig-inal colours and even more to cover the marine growth.

I could not find any texture kits for sale

in stores or online, so I came up with my own design. I will not disclose it now, but some day I will post guides on how to make it on my website, or I will patent the recipe and sell it. I have always been blessed with an eye for anything artistic. I can see details when others might not. My family says that it is common for someone who is deaf because when one sense is gone, the others are stronger. Maybe that is why I focus so much on details.

I am proud and pleased to have completed this model of the *Britannic* wreck. I am not yet finished with my model-ling projects; in fact, I have just started. My next projects are to use 1/144 scale to make both *Titanic* and *Britannic*, but am open to work on projects with others to create a shipwreck model for museums or for other displays.

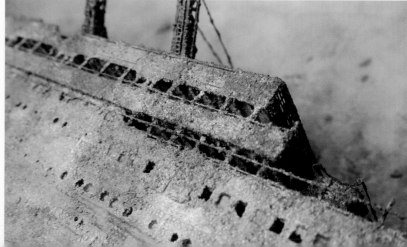

RAISE THE *TITANIC* REPLICA MOVIE MODEL
1/350 scale
By JONATHAN SMITH

Based on the 30-in Minicraft 1/350 scale kit, Jonathan Smith's *Raise the Titanic* movie model is a faithful miniature reproduction of the iconic screen version. The original 1980 film model is still the largest full-scale model of the liner ever built. Made at a cost of £3million with a length of 55-ft, standing 12-ft in height and weighing 10 tons, the model was built on a one piece fibreglass hull, steel superstructure and deckhouses and numerous fibreglass and wood deck details. The film model was built between 1978 and 1979 at the CBS film studios, California, for use in the British ITC movie adaptation of *Raise the Titanic*, based on the 1976 international bestselling Dirk Pitt adventure series novel by Clive Cussler, and the film centred on America's attempt to locate the lost liner. Inside her cargo hold there lies a rare and vital mineral

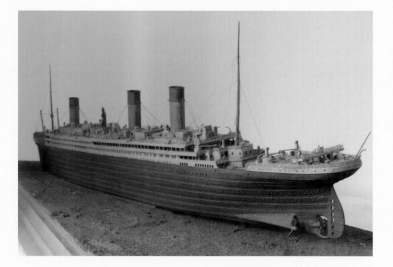

extracted from a mine in Russia in early 1912 and placed onboard the unsinkable liner which could be used to prevent future nuclear wars. It is not only the Americans who want it, but also the Russians, so the race is on to find the wreck. Once she is found, and too far down to access the cargo holds, the Americans have no choice but to raise the *Titanic* and tow her to New York and reveal the cargo hold's secrets.

Due to the size of the model, a special deep water tank was constructed at the film studios, measuring an impressive 348-ft across and 38-ft deep. The *Titanic* model was then connected to a hydraulic arm that was fixed to the base of the deep water tank and when needed, the model could be lifted and lowered at angles to represent the raising of the liner. The film was budgeted at £7million, but with spiralling costs the film finally cost a staggering £25million to make. Sadly, due to the film's Cold War era story-line, and with the real *Titanic* not yet then found but making headlines with numerous attempts to locate her, the film was not well received by the public. To this day, the *Raise the Titanic* film model still resides at the film studios, but having spent three decades exposed .to all weathers, it has virtually disintegrated, rotted and collapsed in on itself with just the one piece fibreglass hull remaining intact.

Because of the state of this film prop, Jonathan decided to replicate it. His miniature version, built in 2003, was taken from the 1998 re-release of the standard Minicraft *Titanic* kit. The kit displays a number of Tom's Modelworks photo-etched detailing sets such as skylights, deck

benches, railings, vent grills, window frames, funnel ladders, compass tower legs, deck steps and cargo crane booms. The solid bulkhead which sits at the tip of the bows was created from brass, along with the sides of the compass tower. The three tall cowling vents, which sit forward and alongside the forward mast, were built from fine plastic doweling rods, cut and inserted into the forecastle deck. The cowl tops were taken from spare vents from an old Airfix 1/600 scale RMS *Mauretania* kit. To mirror the 1980 film model, a number of extra cowl deck vents were added to the replica and placed in the same locations, incorrect on the real *Titanic*. The broken No. 2 funnel on the ship is built from one of the kit's own funnel sets. The other section, which lays on the seabed diorama, is built from another spare funnel set and made to fit perfectly into place with the remains of the funnel on the ship. The photo-etched railings have all been crushed, buckled and twisted in similar style to the movie model. Inside the hull, bulkheads were fabricated from cardboard and cemented into place. These bulkheads can be seen through the iceberg gash cut into the bow's lower starboard side.

After drilling out the hull portholes, the gash in her side was included. Each deck, before being fitted, was built up, covered with scenic evergreen fine model chippings and fine grade sand, and then airbrushed with two shades of matt brown and grey. Each one was then fitted into the hull and the process repeated. With rigging, deck detailing and railings in place, the whole model was sprayed with effect paint known as 'Fleck' that gives smooth surfaces a rough textured feel. As this effect paint was not used to build up the colour and texture of the entire hull, stone chip, spray-on automobile industry paint (used for creating depth in lower panels on cars to prevent

chipping from road surfaces) was also used. The model was then airbrushed grey coated, then layered with three shades of brown, black, white, and finished with matt lacquer.

The diorama base for the model utilised various modelling materials. A wooden base was layered up with various thickness of cardboard. Craft glue was applied and layers of tissue used to build up the thickness of the seabed. While the base was still wet, an old 1/350 hull was pushed into the seabed to form the indentation of where the ship would sit. Once dried, the base was coated in craft glue again and fine scenic chippings, used along with fine builders' sand, were sprinkled onto the base. Extra detail such as gravel was super-glued into position to create boulders and rocks. Craft spray-on glue was then used to seal all the materials together and once dried; the base was painted and then lacquered.

Titanic 1912

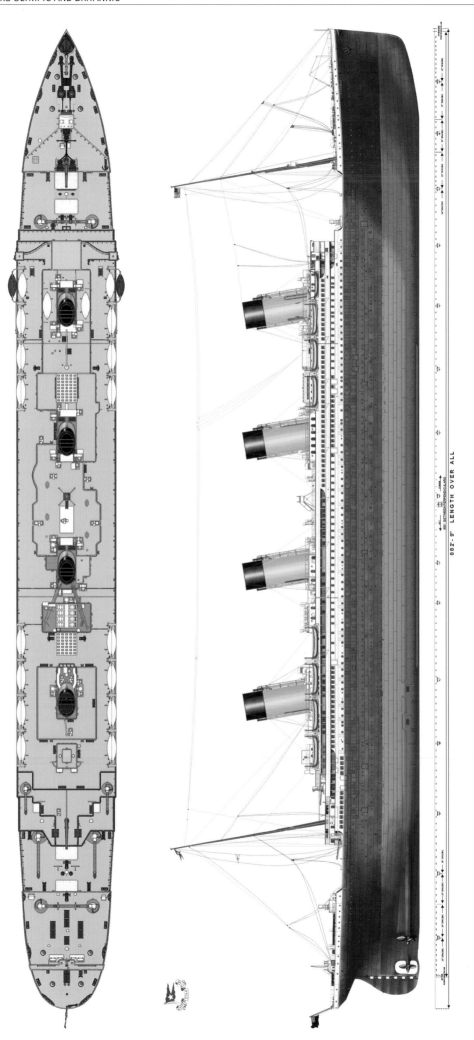

(Drawings by Cyril Codus)

882'-9" LENGTH OVER ALL

Olympic 1911

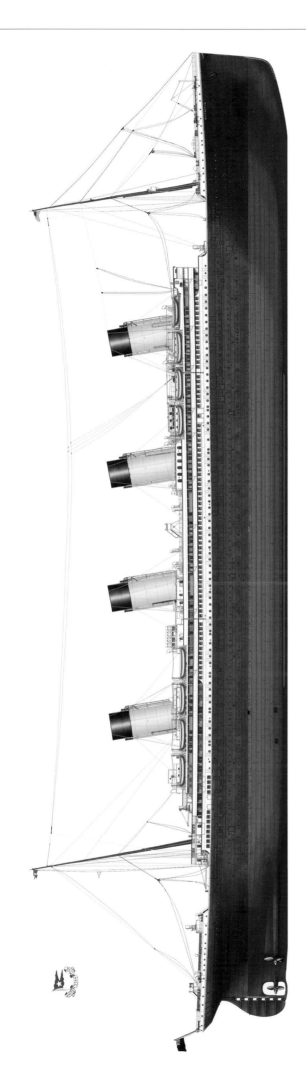

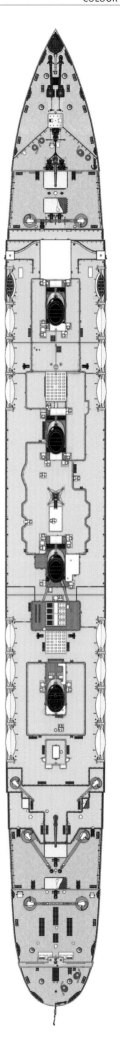

(Drawings by Cyril Codus)

HMT *Olympic* 1918

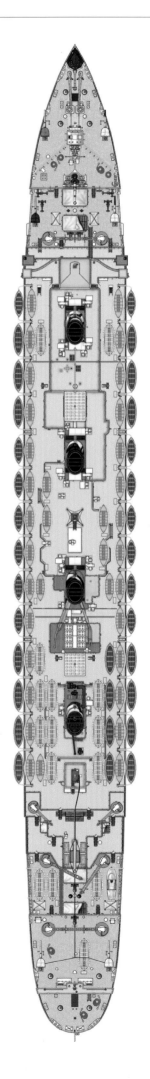

(Drawings by Cyril Codus)

HMHS *Britannic* 1915

(Drawings by Cyril Codus)

Britannic as designed 1914

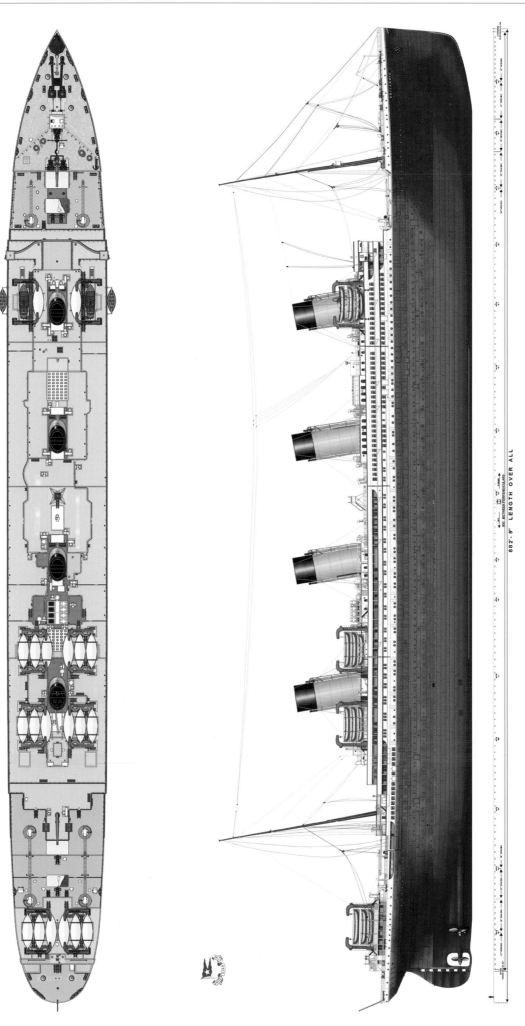

(Drawings by Cyril Codus)

Appearance & Alterations

Even before *Titanic* set sail on her fateful voyage, a number of changes had been made in the design of the two ships. At her launch, *Titanic* was slightly different in minor details to *Olympic*. During the 1912–13 refit at Harland & Wolff, some of these design changes were also extended to *Olympic*.

The first of these changes related to the forward hatch cover. Early in her career, *Olympic* lost No 1 hatch cover in a heavy gale. It was actually bolted to the coaming and weighed some 7 tons, and its loss clearly illustrates the power of North Atlantic seas. While *Titanic* was still under construction, the hatch-coaming facing the bow was angled at 45° to serve as a break-water to prevent the cover from being swept away. This was later changed also on *Olympic*.

Another early difference was that *Olympic* only briefly had Engelhardt collapsible lifeboats installed on the officers' quarters roof as on *Titanic*. These were located on both sides of the first funnel.

The subtle differences in details between the two ships at the time of *Titanic*'s sailing would easily fill a book of this size in itself, so only those details that will be of signifcance to the modelmaker are described here.

The aft grand staircase skylight on *Olympic* had a row of three portholes in its sides; on *Titanic* there were no portholes. The forward grand staircase skylight on *Olympic* also had an arrangement of port-holes in its sides with sliding screens covering them; these were not included on *Titanic*. *Olympic*'s first-class gangway ports on D-deck had portholes, while those on *Titanic* each had two rectangular windows.

Continued on p.53

Olympic's Gymnasium windows.

Above: Taken in June 1911, this image is of *Olympic*'s boat deck looking forward.

Below: Lounge roof port-side looking aft on *Olympic*.

Above: Starboard promenade deck looking aft on *Olympic*.

Below: *Titanic*'s starboard boat deck taken in Queenstown in Ireland.

Above: *Titanic*'s portside boat deck.

Below: Nice candid shot showing passengers on *Olympic*'s B-deck promenade.

Right: An able seaman in the starboard bridge wing cab on *Olympic*.

The tops of the crane bodies on *Titanic* were painted in a shade of grey while those on *Olympic* were white in 1911. The top gunwale of the lifeboats on *Titanic* were a brownish-red; those on *Olympic* were white. These were also changed to red on *Olympic* by May 1912.

The docking bridge on the poop deck of *Titanic* extended over the hull sides (like the promenade deck overhang), while those of *Olympic* ended flush with the hull sides. The tank-room starboard deckhouse side on the boat deck had a single central window on *Olympic*, while there were two on *Titanic*.

These large liners usually underwent annual overhauls in the winter months. It is difficult to determine at which overhaul various alterations actually took place.

Above: A Sunderland Forge and Manufacturing Company electric winch as installed on *Olympic* and *Titanic* in 1911.

Left: After the loss of the *Titanic*, the *Olympic* was fitted out with additional collapsible boats, as can be seen below the conventional lifeboats in this image taken from a White Star Line publicity brochure from before the First World War.

Olympic in wartime dazzle camouflage, one of at least three different schemes she was painted in.

Starboard side view of the same scheme.

After the sinking of *Titanic* and the terrible loss of life involved, *Olympic* underwent several changes to her design, particularly with regard to the arrangement of lifeboats. Immediately after the disaster, *Olympic* received a number of Berthon collapsibles with which the crew were not happy.

In October 1912, *Olympic* was sent back to Harland & Wolff for a substantial refit and was out of service for almost six months. Changes that were not externally visible included the raising of the watertight bulkheads and the installation of an inner skin.

The external changes were, however, very apparent. Her navigating bridge wing cabs were moved further outboard as on *Titanic* (initially these were flush with the promenade deck sides). During this refit, *Olympic* also received a Café Parisienne, as on *Titanic*, and the *a la carte* restaurant was extended to the port side to give these rooms the same window arrangement as on *Titanic*. The most obvious change, however, was the installation of sixty-four lifeboats, of which most were 'nested', with one smaller boat stowed inside a larger boat. To handle these heavy boats, new, larger, electric winches were also installed.

The navigating bridge that had a rounded front on *Olympic* was converted to a flat front as on *Titanic*. Also, on *Olympic*'s

Painters changing the *Olympic*'s camouflage scheme. Note that the portholes have been overpainted.

View of *Titanic*'s flat bridge in Southampton which was to be copied on *Olympic*.

well deck the cargo hatch-coamings were raised to the level of slightly below B-deck.

Long wooden beams were attached underneath the promenade deck overhang, probably to assist in coaling, but these were removed again in the early 1920s. These beams were interrupted at the gangway ports. It seems that at this stage the after well deck's aft bulkhead was completely closed on *Olympic* and received several

Olympic's aft well deck and poop deck in the 1920s

The poop deck on *Titanic*. Here passengers gathered, hoping for final rescue before the ship went down.

watertight doors. Also before the First World War, *Olympic* received a narrow gangway on the port side of B-deck aft leading to the poop deck.

A particular feature that has always confused historians and modelmakers alike is the arrangement of bench seats. The exact location of these was altered many

A group of candid snapshots taken by a passenger onboard the *Olympic* in the 1920s.

times, even when the ships were at sea. I have seen an photograph of *Olympic* with some of the benches even in the aft well deck. It is impossible to determine the exact location of every bench seat at any given time on *Olympic* as well as *Titanic*.

Requisitioned by the Admiralty in September 1915 *Olympic* became His Majesty's Transport 2810 and was used as a fast troopship. In 1916 she was chartered to the Canadian Government and continued to carry troops across the Atlantic from Halifax in Nova Scotia. She was painted with a dazzle camouflage scheme in 1917 and also acquired 6-in guns. The dramatic dazzle scheme is a challenge for any modelmaker.

After the First World War, *Olympic* was converted from a troop transport back to a passenger liner. In the early 1920s, the name *Olympic* on the bows was significantly enlarged and given a greater slant towards the bow and the yellow trim line was moved further downwards to beneath the name. Extra steel panels were attached to the bridge bulwarks to act as breakwaters to prevent spray from soaking those at their stations on the bridge.

In the late 1920s, the cranes were painted in a very dark colour from the top of the bodies upwards. The exact shade is not yet clear, but it might have been black or dark chocolate brown.

In 1929, yet more significant alterations were made on *Olympic* that changed her appearance. Further staterooms were added to the forward part of B-deck, changing the arrangement of windows in this area, and the wireless operator's cabin was moved to the widened Second Class Entrance on the boat deck.

Above: *Olympic* in her happiest days in the 1920s. The seaman on the lounge roof will be marking shuffleboard fields on the deck with chalk, while another seaman is patching up the black paint in the waterway.

Right: With larger, nested lifeboats larger electric winches were required to handle these. Here one of these winches can be seen on *Olympic*'s boat deck during the 1920s.

Above: First Class Smoking Room windows on A-deck

Below: *Olympic* in the final stages of her career. The altered forward B-deck windows can be seen where additional staterooms have been installed.

Above: Verandah Cafe windows on A-deck

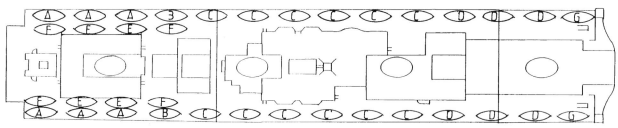

Olympic **Lifeboat Arrangement 1912 – 1918**

A:	Lifeboat	30ft x 9ft x 4ft
	stacked into:	30ft x 9ft x 3ft 7in
B:	Lifeboat	30ft x 9ft x 4ft
C:	Lifeboat	27ft 5in x 8ft 6in x 3ft 7in
	stacked into:	27ft 5 in x 8ft 6in x 3ft 7in
D:	Lifeboat	30ft x 9ft x 4ft
	stacked into:	30ft x 9ft x 3ft 7in
E:	Lifeboat	29ft x 8ft 6in x 3ft 7in
F:	Lifeboat	29ft x 8ft 6in x 3ft 7in
	stacked into	28ft x 8ft x 3ft
G:	Cutter	25ft x 7ft x 3ft
	stacked into:	28ft x 8ft x 3ft

Olympic **Lifeboat Arrangement 1919 – 1934**

A:	Lifeboat	28ft
	stacked into:	30ft
B:	Lifeboat	28ft
	stacked into	30ft
C:	Lifeboat	28ft
	stacked into:	30ft with a 26ft cutter

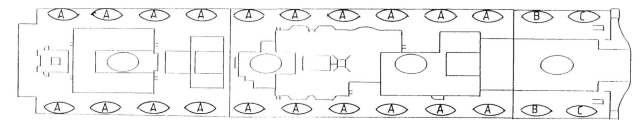

Plans

For many years, Harland & Wolff denied the existence – and thus the availability – of construction plans of its yard numbers 400 and 401, explaining that these were destroyed during an air-raid in the Second World War. I enquired about plans in the early 1980s and received the general arrangement plan that was also published in *The Shipbuilder* in 1911. The copy I have was crudely altered to represent *Titanic*. These plans are largely inaccurate and useless to the serious modeller. I complained, received an apology from the Technical Services department and was told that usually people were perfectly happy with the general arrangement plans. In the large envelope I received was included a superb copy of the 401 rigging plan. During a visit to Harland & Wolff in 1998, I was given a list of all archived plans relating to *Titanic*. This list consisted of some 200 plans and I had sight of all of these. Many, surprisingly, had nothing at all to do with *Titanic* and even included a plan of a motor launch from 1948. Only about twelve plans were eventually of interest to me. Harland & Wolff charged £200 per sheet, irrespective of size, but these plans were of immeasurable technical and historical importance to me and as a result I bought them all. After the closure of Harland & Wolff Technical Services, the material in its archives went to the Ulster Folk and Transport Museum, from which H & W photographs had been long since available. Apparently, due to cataloging delays, the plans are currently not available and will not be for some time.

Robert Hahn (www.Titanic-Plan.de) has computer-drawn a set of plans with the assistance of historian Bruce Beveridge. The set is available in various scales. For years, these plans have been hailed as the best set of *Titanic* plans ever produced, although they are beginning to show their age. The result of the latest research is constantly being added to these plans and Herr Hahn is currently adding the rivet patterns to the steel plates in his side profile. However, Herr Hahn misinterpreted the maximum breadth of 92 ft 6 in (measured at the waterline) as the maximum breadth of the entire ship, which would be the promenade deck. At the promenade deck, the breadth was 94 ft 5 in, and as a result, the hull in the Hahn plans is too narrow. Details such as cowl vents are a little crude. Most modelmakers I know used the Hahn plans together with the author's book *RMS Titanic – A Modelmakers Manual* (Seaforth Publishing) because the plans of fittings in the book are more detailed and much larger than on the Hahn plans.

Very recently, Bob Read from the United States (www.Titanic-cad-plans.com) published a full set of plans, not only of *Titanic* but of also *Olympic* and *Britannic*. The *Britannic* plans are of her both as a hospital ship and as the liner she never was. The plans are exceptionally well detailed (including rivet patterns) and will probably be and remain the last word in *Titanic* plans for a very long time.

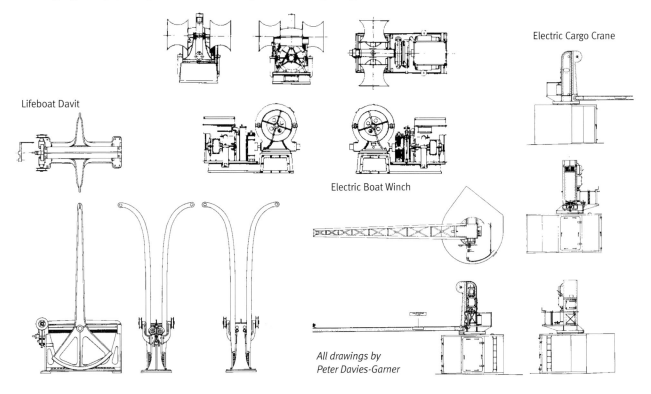

Electric Cargo Crane

Lifeboat Davit

Electric Boat Winch

All drawings by Peter Davies-Garner

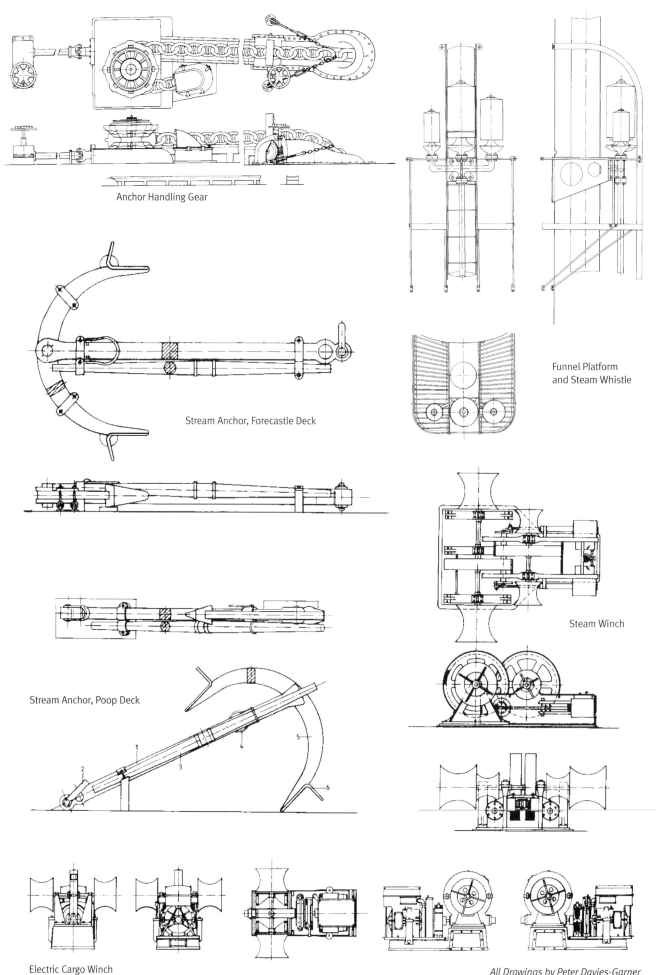

Anchor Handling Gear

Stream Anchor, Forecastle Deck

Funnel Platform
and Steam Whistle

Stream Anchor, Poop Deck

Steam Winch

Electric Cargo Winch

All Drawings by Peter Davies-Garner

RMS *Titanic* 1912

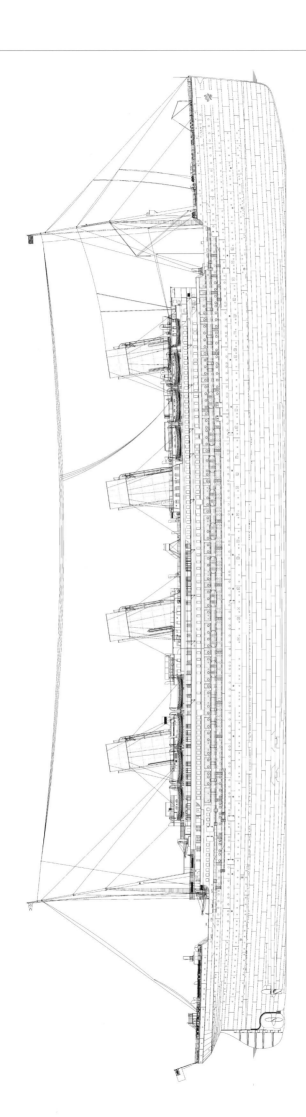

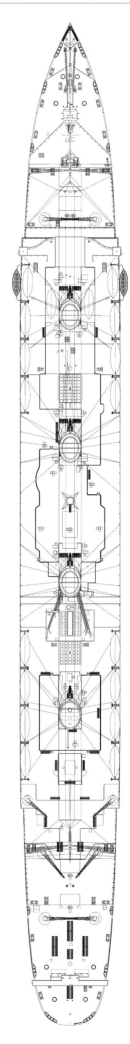

Robert Hahn

Bibliography

The literature on *Titanic* is vast and listed below is a small selection of the most useful to the modelmaker.

Below: This image was taken from a White Star Line publicity brochure from the 1920s. Lifeboats now run the entire length of the boat deck. A boat winch can be seen to the left. The basket-like object mounted on the bulkhead is for stowing a fire-hose, with the nozzle on brackets to the right. This was usually obscured by a bench seat. Bench seats have been placed on the roof of the First Class Smoking Room, showing that they were constantly moved around, even when the ship was at sea.

Archbold, Rick & Ken Marschall, *Ken Marschall's Art of Titanic* (Hyperion 1998)

Ballard, Dr. Robert, *Exploring the Titanic* (Scholastic 1998)

Ballard, Dr. Robert & Rick Archbold, *Discovery of the Titanic* (Warner Books 1998)

Beveridge, Bruce, *Titanic – The Ship Magnificent*, 2 Vols (Tempus Publishing 2008)

Chirnside, Mark, *The Olympic Class Ships* (Tempus Publishing 2004)

Cinefex #72 ,'*Titanic*' Issue (1997)

Davies-Garner, Peter, *RMS Titanic: A Modelmakers Manual* (Seaforth Publishing 2010)

Eaton, John & Charles Haas, *Titanic: Triumph and Tragedy* (Norton 1996)

Hall, Steve & Bruce Beveridge, *Titanic and Olympic: The Truth behind the Conspiracy* (Haverford 2004)

Hutchings, David, *RMS Titanic – 75 Years of Legend* (Kingfisher Railway Productions 1987)

Lord, Walter, *A Night to Remember* (HR & W 1976)

Lynch, Don & Ken Marschall, *Ghosts of the Abyss* (Madison Press 2003)

————, *Titanic: An Illustrated History* (Madison Press 1992)

McCluskie, Tom, *Anatomy of the Titanic* (PRC Publishing 1998)

McCluskie, Tom, Michael Sharpe & Leo Marriott, *Titanic and her Sisters, Olympic and Britannic* (PRC Publishing 1998)

O'Donnell, E E (editor), *Father Browne's Titanic Album* (Wolfhound Press 1997)

Ocean Liners of the Past, Volume 1, 'White Star Triple Screw Atlantic Liners Olympic and Titanic', reprinted from *Shipbuilder Magazine* (PSL 1970)

WEBSITES

www.Titanic-Model.com
www.Titanic-Titanic.com
www.Encyclopedia-Titanica.org